Praise for *Sell Yourself*

This book is a practical "how-to" for creating or repairing your reputation so you don't get in your own way on your climb to the top. Informative and inspiring, Dr. Cindy's "Create. Live. Sell." formula in *Sell Yourself* is the formula to get you where you want to go.

—**Dr. Marshall Goldsmith**, *New York Times* and *Wall Street Journal* #1 bestselling author of *Triggers*

Sell Yourself is the definitive book about how to use personal branding as a personal sales tool. Dr. Cindy draws on her years as a sales consultant and coach to show readers how to use the art of selling to sell themselves. Along the way, she dispels every myth about sales and convinces readers to go after everything they want, need, and deserve in their careers and in life.

—**Dorie Clark**, *Wall Street Journal* bestselling author of *The Long Game* and executive education faculty at Duke University Fuqua School of Business

Personal branding is to networking as networking is to business success. A powerful personal brand is a tool that will help readers make more frequent, deeper connections with people who can help them get ahead. *Sell Yourself* has everything they need to create that powerful brand.

—**Joe Sweeney**, speaker, consultant, and author of *Networking Is a Contact Sport*

You have to believe in you before anyone else will. To build relationships—the key to success—you must first get clear on the value you bring to the table. Dr. Cindy's advice for creating and living a powerful personal brand will help you make strong and lasting impressions on the people you connect with. *Sell Yourself* is a great read for people hoping to expand and strengthen their network.

—**Michelle Tillis Lederman**, author of
The Connector's Advantage and
The 11 Laws of Likability

Cindy McGovern has created a five-step process that anyone can use to apply the skills of the sales professional to any interaction, negotiation, or request. In *Sell Yourself*, she shows readers how important your personal "brand story" becomes in selling yourself both professionally and personally.

—**Mike Bosworth**, author, speaker, and
sales philosopher

Your reputation is one of the most valuable things you have. So why leave it to others to define? Learn how to leave a consistent and positive impression the first time, every time, and with integrity. This, too, is a sales job—and Dr. Cindy is the best person to help you do it with confidence.

—**Ethan Beute**, Chief Evangelist at BombBomb,
host of *The Customer Experience Podcast*,
and *Wall Street Journal* bestselling author
of *Human-Centered Communication* and
Rehumanize Your Business

Life is all about conscious, authentic choices and making the right ones to further our success and growth. It's time to shape our futures with more confidence and clarity. Dr. Cindy's book guides you through that process, with core steps for creating, living, and selling your personal brand so you can make the impact you long to. Embrace your bravery and power, and sell what you love most to share.

—**Kathy Caprino**, author of *The Most Powerful You*, leadership and executive coach, speaker, and senior *Forbes* contributor

Sell Yourself brings a commonsense approach to personal branding and gives the reader many valuable tools. As I transitioned from ice skating to cooking to the opening of my Boitano's Lounges, I could have used Dr. Cindy's beneficial tips.

—**Brian Boitano**, Olympic champion and star of *What Would Brian Boitano Make?*

One of the smartest things a woman can do is brand herself as strong, confident, and reliable. *Sell Yourself* guides the reader through a process to create an authentic, consistent personal brand that will get you what you want, need, and deserve from work and from life.

—**Shelley Zalis**, Chief Troublemaker of The Female Quotient

A carefully crafted personal brand can be a powerful tool when the product you're selling is you. Building and maintaining your reputation and personal brand is key to getting what you want and deserve. *Sell Yourself* takes a unique approach to personal branding that helps the reader embrace the notion that having a good brand is not enough. You have to sell it, and Dr. Cindy teaches you how to sell like a pro.

—**Dr. Marty Seldman**, coauthor of *A Woman's Guide to Power, Presence, and Protection*

Personal branding and reputation management have become must-have skills and Dr. Cindy puts a fresh spin on these important competencies. This time, it's all about selling yourself—with excitement, passion, skill, and courage. Learning to "Create. Live. Sell." your personal brand makes this timeless and timely business imperative easy to grasp, digest, and implement. She teaches you how to differentiate yourself from others with authenticity, creativity, and impact. Part of her distinctive brand is daring to be different, and her writing is informative, clear, and chock full of invaluable tips.

—**Mark Hunter**, host of *The Sales Hunter* podcast and author of *A Mind for Sales*

Everyone has a personal brand. Most people have one by default, but yours must be built by design if you want to take charge of your future trajectory. In *Sell Yourself*, Dr. Cindy McGovern focuses on something many branding books overlook: the importance not only of creating a good brand, but of advocating it into reality. A must-read, great message.

—**Jo Miller**, CEO of Be Leaderly and author of *Woman of Influence*

The "First Lady of Sales" is your offbeat but on-target guru sharing down-to-earth, aha-moment insights while also providing an easy-to-remember, simple model for her subject matter—learning to "Create. Live. Sell." your personal brand to differentiate yourself from others with authenticity, creativity, and impact. This "edu-taining" book is a refreshing, important contribution to the fields of self-help, business, sales, and performance psychology. She not only "lives" her brand, but also she "lives up to it," as she advises. This is Dr. Cindy's workshop-in-a-book, with practical exercises, come-alive examples, clear teaching, and self-reflection opportunities for integrating the self-branding principles and skills into one's life. She's your personal guide and motivational performance coach, helping you to become the world's leading expert on the most important subject in the world—you!

—**Rick Brandon**, PhD, author of *Straight Talk*

I have been in the entertainment business since I was 17. If I were to name one thing that has been absolutely essential to my success, it's the understanding that no matter how much talent I had, I needed to find a way to stand apart from everyone else. Knowing my strengths as well as my weaknesses, my commitment to a strong work ethic, and being almost over-prepared for every performance, have all contributed to my enduring success. This book will guide you in determining whatever it is that makes you unique and going step-by-step to make your dreams a reality.

—**Cavaliere Franc D'Ambrosio**, star of *The Phantom of the Opera*, Hollywood actor, painter/sculptor, and philanthropist

Why create a powerful personal brand if you're not going to sell it? In this value-packed book, Dr. Cindy offers a unique framework for establishing your personal brand and then shows you how to properly amplify it to sell more and serve others. Not only did she pen this book, but she truly lives her message by being her authentic self and allowing her value to sell itself. "Create. Live. Sell." Truly words to live by.

—**Corey Perlman,** owner of Impact Social Media

"Create. Live. Sell." Dr. Cindy offers wonderfully insightful nuggets into how to elevate your brand and sell yourself every day in *Sell Yourself*. With practical concepts like "gracious self-promotion" and "count your facets," you will take away immediate action steps to put into play to develop your brand and close every sale.

—**Dr. Ben Sorensen,** coauthor of *Customer Tells*

SELL YOURSELF

SELL YOURSELF

HOW TO CREATE, LIVE, AND SELL A POWERFUL PERSONAL BRAND

DR. CINDY McGOVERN

NEW YORK CHICAGO SAN FRANCISCO ATHENS LONDON
MADRID MEXICO CITY MILAN NEW DELHI
SINGAPORE SYDNEY TORONTO

1 2 3 4 5 6 7 8 9 LCR 27 26 25 24 23 22

ISBN 978-1-264-84624-5
MHID 1-264-84624-X

ISBN 978-1-264-84931-4
e-MHID 1-264-84931-1

This book is dedicated to you.

Yes - YOU!!

I hope it helps you to create, live and SELL your best self.

Dr. Cindy

Contents

Part Three

Introduction

Personal branding is something people talk about when they refer to curating a social media persona or stepping into a job search for the first time.

It's a question a career counselor or even a friend might ask you. "What's your brand?" It's something we answer with just a few words: "poised and professional," "smart and sassy," "loud and proud," "laid back," "fashion forward."

Most personal branding books will help you arrive at that sort of branding elevator pitch. That's a useful exercise, for sure, but it's just a tiny first step toward creating a brand that will help you sell yourself. This book, *Sell Yourself*, will take you the rest of the way.

The fact is that your personal brand isn't a catchphrase. Say you come up with a personal brand you're happy with, but all you know is how you would like others to describe you. Chances are pretty good, in that case, that you don't really know what your personal brand is at all.

But everyone else does.

And if you have never felt the need to create a personal brand for yourself, you might believe that you don't have a brand or that you don't even need one. But here's the problem with that.

You do have a personal brand, and everyone knows what it is—except for you.

Whether you have taken the time to plan a personal brand or not, you still make an impression on others. When you do, they form an opinion about you. In that moment, they determine for themselves what your personal brand is.

If you have a pithy one-liner that you use to describe your brand, but you don't live up to it every single day, that's not your brand.

The impression you make on others is your brand.

LESSON LEARNED

Let me share something I learned from personal experience as well as from working with thousands of people—both experienced and very young: A personal brand is as complicated and as multifaceted as you are.

It's not something you just say; it's who you are. Your personal brand is you. Or at least it's who and what and how others think you are.

Your personal brand is how you behave, what you say, and how you treat others. It's not only what you say about yourself; it's what others think and say about you, based on how you behave and what you do.

So if your brand is "poised and professional," but you show up at a morning Zoom meeting before you've had a chance to comb your hair or rub the sleep out of your eyes, the impression you make on the others in the meeting is not "poised and professional."

It's "unprepared" or "just woke up" or "Pajamas? Really?!"

That's your personal brand.

That's your personal brand because that's what you sold yourself as when you turned on your camera. That's your personal brand no matter how polished and professional you were yesterday.

What you sell today and every other day is your personal brand.

Sell Yourself will show you how to build the right brand. And it will teach you how to sell it.

I understood how important a personal brand was the minute I realized that if I didn't plan one for myself, live it every day, and sell it to others, others would assign one to me anyway.

That is what they did. And I didn't like the one they chose.

In fact, I learned a tough lesson about what can happen when you leave the work of creating your personal brand to chance.

I was just a few weeks away from graduating with a PhD in communications when a professor I respected and trusted pulled me aside and whispered, "Girls who look like you aren't supposed to be smart."

I was taken aback. Was he referring to my blonde hair? To my free spirit? To my side job as an aerobics instructor? To all of the above?

Yes.

He wasn't trying to insult me. He was trying to show me that this might be a hurdle I would very likely encounter throughout my life. In fact, he was very kindly trying to give me a heads-up that I might need to oversell myself as a smart, capable, ethical researcher and student, starting when I defended my dissertation to the panel of brilliant academics who would decide, in a few weeks, whether I was ready to graduate.

Sure, I'd heard all the "dumb blonde" jokes ever since I was a towheaded kid. And I was well aware that women in general, regardless of hair color, can attract the "wrong" kind of attention—often unwanted. It had happened to me before, even though I tended to dress in buttoned-up, professional clothes.

Yes, I'm blonde. But I'm not dumb. Never have been. I'm curious and resourceful. I've studied my whole life. I learn new skills whenever I can. There's a highly educated brain tucked under my long, blonde curls.

It's like Dolly Parton sings in her famous song "Dumb Blonde": "Just because I'm blonde. Don't think I'm dumb. Cause this dumb blonde ain't nobody's fool."

I know my professor was trying to help me understand an important life lesson: Other people sometimes see us differently from how we see ourselves.

Still, his remark stunned me. He was alerting me in a friendly way that my hard work as an undergraduate, a grad student, and now an accomplished researcher about to finish up a doctoral degree was competing with an age-old stereotype to define me. He was letting me know that others may be buying into those stereotypes linking blonde hair to stupidity. Or they might wonder if I got a step ahead because I used my femininity to convince others to help me or even do my work for me.

My kind professor was letting me know that some people believe "girls"/women like me do just that to succeed. It's how we are sometimes branded. That others might not see beyond the stereotype and recognize my dedication, worthiness, and talents. He was trying to help me understand that despite all the classes I took, I still had one more lesson to learn. I had to do something to change people's minds and destroy their assumptions. At that moment, I realized it was completely in my power to take control of how I'm perceived.

As much as his words shook me in the moment, they led me to an epiphany: *I'm leaving the impression I make on others—to others.*

It's not anyone else's job to decide for me—through misguided assumptions or otherwise—what I'm all about. It's not anyone else's place to pigeonhole me into a "brand" that I haven't chosen or approved.

But because I had never given any thought to branding myself back then, others around me, including those perfectly nice, competent professors and colleagues, did it for me.

If they were basing their perception of me on the stereotypes my professor warned me about, they got it wrong. Dead wrong.

That could have hurt my reputation. It could have held me back from accomplishing my goal of earning a doctorate and becoming a college professor. It could have followed me for a lifetime.

I can't stop people from buying into bogus stereotypes, but I can at least try to stop them from believing I am stereotypical. I realized in that dizzying moment that because I never gave any thought to how others might perceive me—right or wrong—I was leaving the choice up to them.

In short, I was "selling" them on believing whatever they wanted instead of selling them on what I wanted them to believe about me.

Sure, I was in a PhD program—a feat that doesn't happen without a good measure of dedication and intellect. But it's possible that if they bought into any part of that stereotype, that would be enough to make them question my abilities.

I needed a better brand. One that I created on purpose. One that I could use to sell people, including the professors in that room. I wanted them to believe that I was smart, honest, and hardworking enough to earn my own credentials—and to successfully use them throughout my life and career.

I needed a brand that people would buy into, despite the color of my hair. And I needed that brand right now. So I got to work on planning my personal brand.

And then I learned how to sell it.

CREATE. LIVE. SELL.

Sell Yourself will give you the skills you need to create a brand that you can sell—and then to live your brand and sell your brand every day.

Create. Live. Sell. That's my mantra when it comes to personal branding.

My premise: A personal brand is useless unless you do three things:

1. Devote time and thought to planning and creating a brand that you can live up to every day and that will be easy to sell because it's authentically you.
2. Live that brand every day. Everything you do and say leaves an impression on others.
3. Sell your brand. Learn how to sell yourself at work, on job interviews, in your neighborhood, or on the phone with a stranger. Your personal brand is who you are. So it needs to be the sharpest tool in your toolbox when it comes time to sell *you*.

Create. Live. Sell.

The first step—create your brand—seems easier than it is, but because you are a complex, multifaceted person, your brand must also be complex and multifaceted.

The second step—live your brand—is one that many people assume comes automatically. It does not. It's hard work to live up to your brand every time you interact with someone, post something on social media, or shoot off a quick text after having a couple of cocktails or getting some unfortunate news.

And the third step—sell your brand—is one that most people simply ignore, often because it never occurs to them that they need to sell their brand. They don't realize that if they fail to proactively sell their brand, others might not "buy" it. And even worse, others might buy something about them that they never meant to sell at all.

Three steps: Create. Live. Sell.

Sell Yourself is the unique book that looks at personal branding through the lens of sales.

It's shortsighted to create a brand—even a great one—if you're not going to sell it. That would be like plunking down a year's salary on your dream car, but never driving it. *Sell Yourself* is about how to sell your personal brand; that is, how to use your brand to help you succeed and get what you want at work and in life.

Everyone talks about how important it is to "sell yourself," but too many overlook the truly important word in that cliché: "sell."

Sell Yourself puts personal branding into the context of a sales tool. And then it teaches you how to sell.

HOW *SELL YOURSELF* CAN HELP YOU

In the chapters that follow, you will learn how to sell your brand, even if you've never sold anything else.

You will learn that if you don't sell your brand, it will sell itself—and not necessarily in the way that you intend.

"Girls who look like you . . . aren't supposed to be smart."

Not at all what I intended.

By the time you finish reading *Sell Yourself,* you, too, will believe that knowing how to sell like a pro and being willing to sell like a pro are the keys to selling yourself. You will understand the value of selling the personal brand you have created for yourself.

Your personal brand is like a big billboard that advertises the absolute best version of yourself. It lets others know who you are, where you're going, and what your superpowers are. As you sell yourself to bosses, interviewers, colleagues, new friends, life partners, or anyone else who is important to your success in life, your brand is the most important and influential tool in your sales kit.

And yes, selling yourself is a sales job. Literally, when you sell yourself, you make a sale.

Did you just say, "Ick?"

I know, I know. Sales, right? Cheesy. Pushy. Manipulative.

You'd rather do anything but sell, I know. If you wanted to sell, after all, you would look for a job as a sales rep for a big company and pocket those commissions, right? You don't like selling. You don't like being sold. You don't want to have to sell anything, even yourself.

I hear you. That's how I used to feel about sales, too. I don't anymore because I have learned firsthand that sales can and should be a two-way street. A sale should benefit both the person who is selling and the person who might be buying. The sales process can and should be collaborative, honest, and helpful. It should result in a win-win.

That's especially true when it comes to selling yourself by using your personal brand as a sales tool.

To help you sell effectively, I'll share my five-step process for selling your personal brand. It begins with a great plan and finishes with an abundance of gratitude. It's the same process that the most successful sales professionals use every day to sell products and services, and it expands on the sales advice from my *Wall Street Journal* bestselling first book, *Every Job Is a Sales Job.*

Those friendly five steps are:

1. **Plan.** The more thought you put into your personal brand, the easier it will be to live it and sell it. In *Sell Yourself*, we'll dive into two types of plans: one for creating the most authentic brand that will reap you the most success in life, and another for how to sell your brand. You'll learn how to use your personal brand to sell yourself in all sorts of situations, from a job interview to a request for a promotion or raise, to a personal relationship.
2. **Look for opportunities.** If you keep your personal brand top of mind, it eventually will feel natural to use it in any situation that involves an effort to get what you need or want. You can sell your personal brand whenever you see an opportunity that you want to go for. The keys to this step are to recognize those opportunities when they present themselves and to sell your personal brand every time.

3. **Establish trust.** In this step, you listen and observe. Making a sale (even of yourself) is easy when what you're selling will fill a need for the person you're selling to. You can find out what your potential "buyers" need by listening to what they say and observing what they do. For example, if your personal brand is "someone who goes the extra mile" and you learn that your boss needs someone to pitch in on a project over the weekend, pitch in. When you do, you will sell your brand to the very person who will decide whether to choose you for the next promotion that opens up.
4. **Ask for what you want.** This is the hardest step for most people. We're reluctant to ask for a raise or a promotion because we feel our good work should speak for itself. Or we're afraid if we ask, we'll get fired instead of promoted. Neither of those assumptions is valid. A sale rarely happens unless the salesperson comes right out and asks for it. You deserve to have what you want, need, and deserve. It's OK to give yourself permission to go after those things. So ask for them!
5. **Follow up with gratitude.** Gratitude should be part of everyone's personal brand. Selling a brand of gratitude leaves anyone who helped you or even considered helping you with the knowledge that you don't take them, their time, and their effort for granted.

In short, *Sell Yourself* revolves around the three critical components of a successful personal brand:

1. ***Create* your personal brand.** Everyone has a personal brand—even those who say they don't. Those who have not deliberately crafted a personal brand are

simply letting others assume what their brand is. Those assumptions are not always positive.

2. ***Live* your personal brand.** The best way to sell yourself is to thoughtfully and deliberately live the brand you have created, day in and day out.
3. ***Sell* your personal brand.** *Sell Yourself* will teach you how to sell your personal brand like a pro, using my five-step sales process. Whether you are a seasoned sales pro or someone who does not sell for a living (and doesn't want to), you can and do sell every day, so you might as well do it the right way.

Sell Yourself will help you if:

- You're young and eager to begin creating and selling your personal brand.
- You believed you already had adopted the perfect brand but have found it is not working for you—perhaps because you're not selling it.
- You're stuck at work or in life, and you're ready to move on, but your brand isn't getting you anywhere.
- You're inadvertently selling the wrong thing.

Sell Yourself will prove equally valuable whether you are new to personal branding, you have experimented with personal branding, or you are at a juncture in life when your personal brand needs a serious makeover.

Professional salespeople know the key to successful selling lies in the way they present themselves to others—that is, in the way they brand themselves and sell their brands. That is also the key to getting what you want, need, and deserve.

I hope you will enjoy the stories I tell in *Sell Yourself* about my own journey with personal branding and the examples I have written about my clients and acquaintances who have let me help them create their personal brands.

I hope my book will help you embrace the need to sell your brand—to sell you—and the value of selling like a real pro. Mostly, though, I hope *Sell Yourself* will lead you to the success you want in your life—both at work and personally.

SELL YOURSELF

PART ONE

1

Create. Live. Sell.

Think of someone who is unforgettable.

It might be a dear-departed grandmother, a superstar where you work, or a best friend who is always there for you. It could be a star athlete, an inspiring author, or a celebrity who seems to do no wrong.

What is it about that person that is so memorable? What comes to mind when someone mentions the person's name?

Chances are good that it's something specific, something you can describe in just a couple of words. There's something the person does that is so consistent, it's like a trademark. It's something reliable, something you absolutely know about the person, something you could describe using the word "always," as in, "She always makes me feel welcome" or "He always looks sharp."

A great example is Dolly Parton.

She always looks the same: big blonde hair and a bigger smile. Thin yet curvy. Sparkly clothes. High-heeled shoes. She always acts the same: Full of sass. Funny. Humble. Mega-talented.

That look, that personality, that voice: They're her trademarks. They never change. You can count on them. She never waivers from them.

Seriously, never. She's been quoted so many times saying she doesn't wash the makeup off her face before she goes to sleep in case she's jolted out of bed and onto the street by a fire or another emergency. She doesn't want the firefighters or the onlookers to catch even a glimpse of her naked from the neck up, without her heavy makeup or teased blonde wig.

Dolly Parton wouldn't be Dolly Parton without that heavy makeup and a teased blonde wig.

She knows it. You will never, ever see her look like anything but the Dolly Parton you think you know. You can count on that. She lives that look. She lives that trademark. It's her signature.

It's her personal brand.

It's not something she created so she could describe herself that way to others. It's not an image she created just for marketing posters and album covers and concerts. It is quite literally who she is, day in and day out.

Yes, Dolly Parton is, indeed, her own creation. And every day since she decided to present Dolly Parton to the world with a signature look and personality as unmistakable as her Grammy-winning soprano, she has lived that creation. And she has sold that version of Dolly Parton to the world to the tune of $600 million, her net worth in 2021.

What have you created for yourself? What do people say that you "always" do or "always" present yourself as? What is your signature, your trademark? What are you selling about yourself to others?

In short, what is your personal brand?

Dolly Parton's personal brand is one of the most successful in the world because she has done three things with it: She created it with intention. She lives it consistently. She uses it to sell herself to the public.

Create. Live. Sell. One without the others is not a powerful personal brand.

If you create a brand but do not live it, you've got a slogan or a wish, not a brand. If you create a brand and don't use it to sell yourself, you've got little more than a to-do list whose items you never checked off.

And if you're living a brand that you have not thoughtfully created, focused, honed, and tested, you really don't know what you're selling, do you?

Combining three personal branding actions (Create. Live. Sell.) will make you unforgettable. It will make your brand unmistakable so nobody will assume you are something you don't intend to be. It will make you more successful at work and in your life because it will help you present yourself as the person you want others to see and know.

CREATE

Like all things in life, your personal brand will be more successful—and so will you—if you spend time planning it.

Think about the last project you did at work that turned out exactly as you wanted. Did you dive into it headfirst without considering how much time it would take you, when you would find that time, who might be able to help you, whether you had a budget for it, and what your boss's vision was for it?

Nope.

When we start anything without a good plan, we tend to flounder. We thrash around trying this and that until something works. Where I come from, we call that "throwin' spaghetti at the wall and seein' what sticks."

Throwing spaghetti at the wall is a big waste of time. Writing a term paper without first doing the research is going to take you twice as long as one that you started after you gathered your information, made an outline, and cleared your schedule. Going to the grocery store without making a meal plan for the week and writing down a list of needed ingredients means you'll have to make extra trips to the market every time you start cooking. Hopping on a plane to Europe without planning your trip will very likely leave you unable to enjoy the shows, restaurants, and hotels that are already booked up by travelers with the good sense to make reservations months in advance.

The same goes for your personal brand. You can't wing it. You have to plan your brand. You have to intentionally create your brand, or it might not stick. Even worse, others might assume your brand is something entirely different from what you think it is—and *that* might stick.

Then you'll have to spend your time undoing that damage and—it is my hope—you will then hunker down and do the work of creating a brand that you can live every day and that you can use to sell yourself in the precise manner that will get you exactly what you want, need, and deserve.

When you take the time to create a personal brand that reflects who you truly are and who you intend to become, you take control of your own story. When you give serious thought to how you want others to think about you, experience you, talk about you, and remember you, you control the narrative.

You leave your reputation up to you, not to others.

Just as importantly, creating a thoughtful, deliberate brand will become a road map for your behavior and choices, from the company you keep, to what you say to whom, to the way you dress and present yourself in every situation. If you think deeply enough about the brand you create, it will stop you from doing, saying, or engaging in things that could lead people to think about you in a light other than the one you want to shine on yourself.

Like Dolly Parton, you can become your own creation. If you are satisfied with yourself just as you are, a well-planned personal brand can help you stay the course as you consistently show up as authentic and comfortable in your own skin. If you'd like to stretch into territory that is somewhat unfamiliar, careful planning can result in a brand that shows others you belong there. If you want to completely turn the boat around and go in a new direction, you'll first need to consider how to do that, whether you can pull it off, and what changes or sacrifices it will require.

You might believe it is unnecessary to carefully create a personal brand that shows the world your absolute best. You can simply show the world your absolute best without a plan, right?

Sure, sometimes.

But if you want to achieve your goals, random won't get you there. Neither will inconsistency, uncertainty, or luck.

Just ask Dolly.

LIVE

How many prized possessions do you ignore because they're tucked away on a shelf or in a cabinet or even out of sight in a closet?

Maybe you're happy to own them and having them is enough. They don't really do anything for you except perhaps make you smile every now and then when you pull them off the shelf to dust them or show them off to visitors. They don't have any useful purpose. They don't get you anything.

If you go to the trouble to create a personal brand but you don't use it, on the other hand, having it is most definitely not enough.

If you make the effort to curate and craft a brand but you don't follow through on it, do you really have a brand? Or at least, do you really have the brand that you took the trouble to create?

You can dust your brand off and reread the rationale that went into it, and it might rev you up for a while. You can show off your brand by telling others what it is. You can know that you created a brand and all the facets that are part of it. You can write your brand down and keep it in a safe place.

But that kind of brand doesn't have any useful purpose. It doesn't help you reach your goals.

Creating a brand with no intention of incorporating it into your everyday life—of *living* it—is a futile exercise and a waste of time.

What if Dolly Parton had created the brand of a flashy country singer with mile-high bleached blonde hair recognizable to everyone in the world with just a glance—but then chopped off her long locks, became a brunette, dressed in baggy blue jeans, and skipped the makeup except when she was on stage?

Her brand would be "plain, just for show, and rumpled."

What if you created the brand of an "energetic, polished professional" but wore tattered sneakers to the office and barely spoke up in staff meetings, except on days when the CEO was scheduled to meet with your team?

Your brand would be "passive, kiss-up, and unprofessional."

No brand, no matter how well planned, is *your* brand until you live it every day.

You can't write a brand down on a piece of paper, or tell others what your brand is, or label yourself with branding words and expect everyone to believe any of it if that's all you do.

In other words, creating a personal brand doesn't finish the job. Creating the brand is only Level 1 of the three-tiered branding process: Create. Live. Sell.

Creating a brand but not living it is like writing out invitations for a dinner party, planning the menu, researching recipes, buying the ingredients, and taking the day off from work to prepare, but never sending the invitations or cooking the meal.

It's like planting a tree but never watering it; writing a book but never showing the manuscript; registering for classes but never going to campus or even logging in.

You might get a smidgeon of benefit from each of those exercises, but you won't get a lush umbrella of shade on a hot day, or your name on the cover of a bestseller, or a diploma.

The plan won't execute itself. The intention alone won't put your best foot forward. And the creation of a personal brand doesn't mean that's your brand.

Not unless you follow through. Not unless you bring it to life by living it.

How do you live it? You live up to it. You live like it's who you are. You live like you *are* the brand.

Of course, you're not the brand. The fact is, the brand is *you*.

Living a personal brand means never—or at least oh so rarely—deviating from the qualities you have decided you want to show to the world. If your brand is "nice," then be nice. If you're not nice, you'll blow your brand. If your brand is "go-getter," then go get 'em. If you slack off, refuse challenges, and make excuses, your brand will be the opposite of go-getter.

You can choose your brand, but if you don't live it, you invite others to override your choice. Others will brand you as "not nice" the minute you behave that way. From then on, that's your brand, no matter how much time and effort you put into your branding plan.

Living your brand means speaking, behaving, and even dressing and existing in a way that is consistent with the qualities you have chosen to brand yourself with. It means resisting the urge to say or do something that contradicts those qualities. It means being on guard at all times so you don't slip. It means knowing your brand so well that adhering to it is automatic, authentic, and easy.

Or at least it becomes easy over time.

When you commit to living your brand, you make a pact with yourself. You have done the creative legwork to fashion a brand that not only suits the real you but can position you to achieve whatever is next for you.

Living your brand is like keeping a promise to yourself to be your best self so you can live your best life. It's an awareness that if you are not true to your brand, your dreams are unlikely to come true.

If you want to live your dreams, then live your powerful brand.

SELL

When you truly live your brand, it's easy to sell it.

Selling your personal brand is the best way to sell yourself. Finish this sentence: "I want to sell myself as ________."

Do you want to sell yourself as a dependable employee? A respected leader? A social media influencer? A good parent?

The words you filled in are the essence of your brand. If you want to sell yourself as a reliable, careful house cleaner who is worth paying top dollar for, then create a brand that gets you there, and then live that brand.

Your brand might include a plan to always be on time to the homes of clients; to own up to it if you break something—but to take every precaution so you won't have to. Your brand might involve cleaning the homes of others as thoroughly as if your own family lived there. Your brand might revolve around doing more than other part-time house cleaners are willing to do, like ironing or washing windows or cleaning the oven—for an upcharge, of course. Your brand might include being friendly to clients and their families.

Every time you live up to your own brand, you sell it. In the house cleaner scenario, you're selling yourself as reliable, careful, honest, friendly, thorough, and willing to do more. Those aren't just claims; you prove that your brand is authentic every time you walk into a client's home. You give your clients a reason to say you "always" arrive on time; you "always" go the extra mile; you're "always" trustworthy.

When those clients list your "always" credentials in conversations with their neighbors, those neighbors are going to want you to clean their homes, too. Chances are good that they have experienced house cleaners who maybe aren't always professional, consistent, responsible, and trustworthy. Chances are good that those neighbors are willing to pay extra to someone who is.

What has happened is that those neighbors have bought what you sold them. You branded yourself as a competent, dependable house cleaner, and that's what they were looking to buy. They had a need, and they believed you could fill it. So they hired you to fill it.

That's what a sale is.

ALWAYS, NEVER

Give this exercise a try.

Write down five words or phrases that you would like others to associate with you. Then see if you can write "always" or "never" before any of them.

Examples:

always—on time.
always—keep my promises.
never—raise my voice.

All sales are based on trust. You'll never sell anything—including yourself—without first establishing trust. When you create a brand based on your finest qualities and you live up to those qualities every day, you have a brand that leads others to trust you. Sell that brand. When you sell that brand, you sell yourself.

Think of your personal brand as a sales tool. Think of living your brand as making a sale. What you're selling is you—the same you that your brand says you are.

Celebrate those sales. I can't tell you how many clients and friends I've known who have felt like they were bragging or even downright dirty for branding themselves based on their awesome qualities and then using those brands to get something they want: a job, a raise, a new client, a sale.

They believe salespeople are manipulative and dishonest. They don't want to come across that way by selling a brand that only showcases their best qualities. What they might not realize, though, is that when you live and sell your best self, that's good for others, too.

It's a win-win kind of sale. What's the least bit dirty about that?

2

Know What You Are Selling

Most of us know someone like the remarkable young woman I'm about to describe. I'll call mine Bikini Girl. Yes, I know that's a bit insulting. You'll understand the nickname as you read on.

This Bikini Girl is brilliant. She got straight As in college. She makes friends easily. She has great ideas and she's not afraid to act on them. If she fails, she tries again. She's bold. She's interesting. She's talented. She's reliable. She's going places.

She's also tall and sexy, and she's into fashion.

She wants to be a documentary filmmaker. Or a model. Or a social media influencer.

I can't tell.

She has two Instagram accounts. On the first one, over the past year, she has posted 365 photos of herself wearing bikinis. Skimpy ones. A different bikini every single day. Other photos show her in clingy minidresses, or skin-tight jeans and lacy bralettes, or a bare midriff, or a micro-miniskirt, or short-shorts. Her velvety auburn hair is usually in her face. Her eyes say, "I know I'm hot."

On her second account, her profile picture shows a serious young professional with perfect hair, perfect makeup, a humble smile, and eyes that say, "I'm polished, capable, and professional." Her weekly posts on this account lead readers to a YouTube channel full of amazing, professional video interviews she has done with young people with extraordinary accomplishments, incredible stories, or salient advice.

In each video with an interviewee, she's dressed in fairly conservative business-casual clothes. The interviews are perfection. The videos are well-edited.

I can't help but wonder if she knows that her two groups of followers can see both accounts. That a potential documentary employer can see Bikini Girl? And that someone who has seen both accounts calls her Bikini Girl and not Documentary Filmmaker?

Both are strong brands, but this talented young woman is living with an unanswered question: "What am I selling?"

It seems that she has no clue.

She can't decide which brand to sell, so she sells both, and they contradict each other.

The first step in creating a brand that you can sell is to know—for sure—what that brand is. In fact, the first step in selling anything is to know which product you're selling—and why.

If your product is you, it seems you would know what you're selling. But Bikini Girl isn't alone with this sort of split-personality brand.

She has a decision to make: Which version of her brand does she want to sell? The answer to that will come once she decides exactly what she wants from her career and her life.

And that, like all good sales, starts with a plan.

HOW TO CHOOSE A BRAND YOU CAN SELL

The most important thing you will ever sell is yourself. Your brand is your most effective sales tool.

So to sell yourself, you have to sell your personal brand.

You sell your brand 24/7. You sell it by the way you carry yourself, the way you dress, the way you speak to others, the things you say to them, the way you react to them. And yes, you sell it by what you post on social media.

What are you selling? Is it the best "you" you can be?

Is it immediately clear, when you meet others, what you're selling? Is it perfectly clear what your brand is?

Is it the brand that is going to get you what you want and where you want to be?

Do you *know* what you want and where you want to be?

Aah. Let me ask you that again: Do you know what you want and where you want to be?

Like Bikini Girl, many people cannot answer yes to that question. And until you can, you will have trouble creating and selling a brand that gets you what you want and where you want to go.

The reason I don't know if Bikini Girl wants to be a documentary filmmaker, a model, or a social media influencer is because she doesn't know. Until she figures that out, she won't be able to create a brand that helps her sell herself as one of those things. Until she figures that out, people who might be willing to help her get there really can't do anything for her.

That's not to say people are one-dimensional. Bikini Girl is definitely talented. It's possible she could use her talents to make a career in any of a number of fields.

But few people juggle multiple, competing careers at once. Bikini Girl needs to narrow it down. She needs to choose. She needs to create a focused personal brand that will help her make her mark. She needs to be something, not everything. She needs to know what she's selling.

Until then, she's selling a brand that says, "I don't know what I want to be. I don't know who I am. I don't know what I'm selling."

This reminds me of a restaurant I once saw called "Thai-Mex." I never went because I couldn't decide what I wanted to eat and that name wasn't making it easy for me to decide.

If Bikini Girl doesn't know what she wants, how can she get it? If she doesn't know what she wants, how can others help her get it?

MAKE A CHOICE

Bikini Girl isn't the only person I know who is selling a brand of confusion.

A young computer salesman lost 50 pounds, bulked up, earned his personal trainer certificate, and created a web page and some dedicated social media accounts to promote his side hustle as a trainer. He hopes to build that business into a full-time career, without quitting his sales job first. So he spends much of his time at his computer sales job trying to sell his training services rather than his company's products. His department head told him his side business is damaging his credibility as a product salesman. The salesman wants to do both until his training business takes off, but he's splitting his brand, and it could cost him his primary source of income.

An aspiring actress with a college degree in information technology took a job with a big electronics store chain fixing laptops and advising customers about which equipment to buy for their home offices. She's able to schedule her store shifts so she has free time to go to auditions. At the store, however, her manager has overheard her telling clients, "I'm not really a computer person. I'm an actress." Some of the customers have asked for a different advisor, saying they don't believe an actress has the experience or knowledge to help them choose. The actress needs a paying job until she gets a good role, but her conflicting brands have damaged her credibility at the store.

A kindergarten teacher who's in her first year of teaching loves children, wants to have lots of them herself, and has wanted to work with them since she was a teenager. She also loves to have fun on the weekends and to post social media photos of herself partying and posing with friends. Her principal has seen the photos and warned the teacher that her after-hours life poses a conflict of interest for someone who works with children. The teacher assured the principal that her privacy settings prevent the kids from finding out. But it didn't stop the parents, who complained so much that the teacher lost her job.

None of these well-intentioned young people ever intended their after-hours brands to affect their success at work. But they did.

Mixed messages diminish and dilute your brand.

There's no harm in showing a fun side or letting others know your interests, even at work, as long as it doesn't ruin your reputation.

The computer salesman, for example, could limit his efforts to sell training services to after hours and to clients who are not affiliated with his day job. The actress certainly could share her excitement about her auditions with coworkers but keep it all business with customers. And the kindergarten teacher really needs to choose career over lifestyle if she wants to work with children. No parents are going to be comfortable with sending their kids into a classroom with a teacher who showcases how much she parties.

Likewise, Bikini Girl could continue to show off her lithe figure by wearing her skimpy outfits to festivals and the beach—without making her body the centerpiece of her social media presence. She can incorporate the fun side of her personality into a whole-person brand that she can "sell" to clients, bosses, and new friends, who might "buy" her as more professional and credible than they do now when she is pushing the fun part of her brand so hard on social media.

WHAT DO YOU WANT?

In the next chapter, I'll show you a manageable way to carefully plan your brand so you can create one that you can sell.

First, though, let's spend some time figuring out what, exactly, you want your brand to be.

I'm a born planner, so I'm usually pretty clear about what I want. Still, my plans have changed over the years. At one point, I sold a brand as a fitness instructor. Along the way, I've sold myself as a student, a researcher, a professor, a sales consultant, a trainer, and now an author.

Sometimes I've sold myself as more than one of those things, but that doesn't mean I had separate, or contradictory, brands. My brand isn't just about *what I do*. Instead, it's about *who I am*: hardworking, smart, curious, helpful, kind, independent, always learning.

I don't brand myself as a full-time fitness instructor anymore. I brand myself as an author, speaker, and entrepreneur running a successful business consulting firm. Yet my brand is basically the same now as it was when I was teaching at the gym. At the core of my brand as a fitness instructor were my qualities as hardworking, smart, curious, helpful, kind, reliable, and independent. At the core of my brand as a business owner are those same qualities.

I still love fitness. I also like to dance. I'm in love with my little dog, Biscuit. I'm a fan of scary movies.

In short, I'm a multifaceted person, just like you. But I don't let my many facets compete with each other.

Posting bikini pics of myself on social media would fragment my brand. It would be off brand for me. That doesn't mean I can't or wouldn't wear a bikini to the beach with my family or friends.

In fact, if Bikini Girl knew for sure that she wanted to be a model and not a documentary filmmaker, then her Instagram Stories would make perfect sense and would sell the brand she wants people to buy. But those photos might interfere with her success if she decides to go into a more conservative profession. Once she makes that decision, she can start using her Instagram posts to sell the people who might like to hire her on her qualifications for her future profession.

A lot of people struggle with reconciling the many facets of their brand, possibly because they, like Bikini Girl, haven't figured out who they are—and what they want to "sell" others on—at their core.

I love the sweet movie *The Holiday*, which stars Jude Law as a widowed dad. He strikes up a romance with Cameron Diaz's character, but doesn't tell her he has children.

When she asks him why he kept that from her, he says he tries to be just one thing at a time because he doesn't know how to turn off the "dad" in him when it's time to be a "date."

He doesn't know how to incorporate his many facets into one brand, but it's truly not that hard. At the character's core is a nice guy who cares about people and loves his kids. He also wants to find a nice woman.

We all have to figure out how to blend our interests in a way that allows them to complement each other rather than compete with each other.

Bikini Girl/Documentary Filmmaker's two brands are competing with each other.

Can you give your brand just one name? If not, is that because you're trying to "sell" two completely different brands? That just won't work.

Here's an idea that just might work: Find a middle ground that allows you to live a brand that lets you authentically express yourself in a way that won't hinder your success. Maybe that means you should keep your wild side private rather than posting it all over Twitter. Maybe it means taming your impulses so they don't get in the way of your success in your career and your life. Or maybe it means fully embracing one or the other of your two personas and letting the other one go. Maybe it means elevating different parts of your personality and your brand for different audiences in different situations.

It all comes down to deciding who you are and what you want. Until you figure out what you're selling, though, you won't be able to sell it.

I made those decisions for myself after I got over the shock of hearing, "Girls who look like you aren't supposed to be smart" in graduate school. Remember my story from the Introduction of this book?

I know that I have to sell a brand—smart, capable, professional—that other people might not immediately buy because they believe in stereotypes. So, I don't engage in behaviors that would raise eyebrows that I don't want to raise.

I know what I'm selling, and I sell that—and nothing else. I know what my brand is, and I live it.

I would never tell people—not even Bikini Girl—that their brands are no good for them. That's up to them to decide. But I would urge them to decide, because trying to live and sell two completely different brands at the same time is going to cause problems for them on both ends. They need to take inventory and get feedback from trusted friends. And then choose one or the other.

Until they do, they will continue to leave that choice up to others. They're simply selling too many things for it to be clear to anyone else exactly what they're selling—or who they really are.

CAN'T DECIDE?

If you're stuck between two brands because you haven't decided exactly what you want, ask yourself five questions:

1. What does success look like for you?
2. What are the qualities you want others to know you for?
3. What do people think when they hear your name? Is that what you want them to think?
4. What are you doing now that might prevent people from thinking about you the way you would like them to? What information is out there that contradicts this? What are you doing that could give people an impression that is opposite from the one you want them to have?
5. What brand do you believe will get you what you want from your career and life?

Sales professionals understand that they can't sell products or services if they don't know what they're selling. Before they ever approach a potential customer, they spend time getting to know their products, how those products will be perceived by others, what objections they may encounter, and how to best position the products to the customer.

Likewise, you can't sell yourself if you don't know what you're trying to sell. To use a sales term, you need to know the "FAB"—features, advantages, and benefits—of your product, which is you.

Don't leave your brand to others—or to chance. Think through what your brand will be. Make some serious decisions about the impression you want others to have about you. Spend some time figuring out how to cultivate that image and how to stick to it so your behavior, style, social media posts, and reputation are consistent.

Spend some time deciding what you're selling. Create a plan around how you want others to view you. If you were to overhear colleagues, clients, or new acquaintances talking about you, what would you like them to say? Figure that out, and the best brand for you will become obvious.

3

Plan Your Brand

Every successful sale begins with a good plan. So does every successful personal brand.

Your personal brand is how people see you. It's what you're known as and what you're known for. It's the impression you give others—first impressions and lasting impressions. It's what you're selling about yourself to others.

So it's important to very deliberately think through what your brand will be. It's important to make serious decisions about the impression you want others to have about you, and then spend some time figuring out how to cultivate that image and how to stick to it so your behavior, style, social media posts, and reputation are consistent and reinforce that brand.

Inconsistency is probably not the brand you're trying to create for yourself.

So create a plan around how you want others to view you.

Choose and fine-tune and shape your personal brand into a blueprint for the way you carry yourself, the way you dress, the way you speak to others, the things you say to them, the way you react to them.

Every good salesperson understands that you have to know your product inside and out and make a plan to sell every aspect of it.

How much more powerful or successful or guaranteed would you be at selling yourself if you had a plan for how you speak to others, what you say, and how you react?

That might seem unnecessary. You're *you*, after all. You speak how you speak. You react how you react.

But if you truly want to make a specific impression on others, can you really count on yourself to say and do the right thing all the time?

People who spend time and considerable thought planning just how they must behave in order for others to see them the way they want to be seen are more likely to make the impression they desire. Those who rely on their natural charm and nice personality without crafting a thoughtful personal brand have a harder time consistently portraying themselves the way they want to be perceived.

That's because we all have our moods. We have good days and bad days. Sometimes we know just what to say and how to react, and sometimes we're caught off guard. Sometimes others push our buttons. Sometimes we simply lose it.

Plan how you will present yourself in those situations.

Often this comes naturally. If you have to have a difficult conversation with a boss or a friend, for example, you would spend some time planning the conversation, right?

Sometimes if we don't research, think through, and plan our personal brand, we might misunderstand what kind of communication or actions are called for as we interact with others on our way to achieving our goals.

A plan can help us avoid those mistakes.

I'm not saying that missteps will magically never happen again if you invest time and thought in a personal branding plan. But they will happen far less often if you take the time to think through how you will uniformly behave, no matter what the situation.

BRAND PLANNING CHECKLIST

The most effective way to start building your personal brand is to make a plan. Here is a checklist to get you started.

1. Identify the "You" That You Want to Present to the World

As we saw in Chapter 2, placing equal priority on multiple facets of your personality and ambitions can lead to a brand that is confusing to others and stifles your ability to show your best self consistently.

As we'll discuss in Chapter 11, people are multifaceted, and so are brands. But at its core, a personal brand is a guide for presenting yourself in a very specific way that will help you to achieve very specific goals.

Start with how you identify yourself in the world. For example, is your religion an important part of who you are? How strongly do you identify with your race, ethnic origin, gender, sexual orientation, or social class? Those sorts of demographic characteristics—your "social identity"—could become part of your brand, depending on how relevant or important you feel they are to achieving your goals in life.

As you move into creating your brand, however, you will spend a lot of time examining your goals, feelings, talents, and personal qualities. You will answer this all-important question: Who are you at your core?

If you can align the answer to that question with your goals, you can create a personal brand that will feel natural to live day in and day out and that will get you closer to achieving your dreams.

Here is an activity that will help you determine your core values, which will become the foundation of the brand you build.

IDENTIFY YOUR CORE VALUES

Identifying the values that are important to you to live your best life is a useful exercise. Companies do that all the time: Their leaders figure out what their company's mission and values are and incorporate those into all the brands they sell.

Knowing what is most important to you will help you take that into consideration whenever you make a decision; in how you treat other people; in what you go after in life. It also will help you understand your own reaction to others who might have different values because they come from different cultural or educational backgrounds. Knowing your core values is key to creating a personal brand that is authentically you.

Start by finding a private, quiet place to think and write. Then answer these questions:

- Who is the person you most admire in your world, living or dead? Choose someone you know/knew personally.
- What are 15 words that describe what you admire most about that person? Keep thinking until you have 15 words. Write them down.
- Changing course, what is the best moment of your life that you can remember? Or a very favorite memory?
- Why was it so memorable and wonderful? Write down 15 words that describe how great it was.
- Look at the 30 words you wrote down. Look for words that mean almost the same thing. Put them into a group. Give the group a name that is only one word. For example, if you wrote "honest," "authentic," and "sincere," put those in a group and call it "honesty." Narrow your list down to 10 groups of two to five words and be sure each group has a one-word title. Write each title on another part of your page.
- Study those 10 titles. Which five of those one-word titles best describe your truth? Choose the five that tell the story of who you are in your heart and how you hope others see you. Let the other five go.

The five words you have left are your core values.

Now consider why those five values are so important to you:

- Identify the people and situations that influenced you in developing your values.
- Then thoughtfully answer this question: How can you rely on those values to guide you as you make decisions about what to say, how to behave and react, whom to associate with, and which career/relationships/lifestyle to go after?

This is an exercise in awareness. You might be surprised more by what's not on the list than by what is. Examining that list might help you realize that you've been chasing goals that aren't important to you or right for you. Keeping that list in front of you—say, taping it to your computer, carrying it in your wallet, or saving it in a note on your phone—is a handy way to gauge how the decisions you make will reflect your values.

And making it your central reference point as you plan the personal brand you want to live and sell will help you focus on what's truly important to you in terms of what you want to achieve, how you want to live your life, and how others perceive you.

Companies that have strong brands identify the organization's core values. Some, like the Ritz-Carlton, even ask their employees to carry a laminated list of those values with them.

2. List Your Big Life Goals

What is your dream career? Do you want to spend your life with a partner? Have children? Devote yourself to the service of others? Become wealthy? Turn your hobby into a business? Travel the world? Bring an invention to life?

Here's another activity: In your mind, imagine yourself 20 years from now, happy and fulfilled. Don't worry about what's possible or realistic. Don't put any financial or other practical limits on your imagination. Don't factor in obligations that might arise, like the need to live in a certain place to be close to a sick relative, for example. Just pie-in-the-sky it.

What do you see? Is that what you want? What do you have to do now to get there?

How do you have to present yourself to the world in the context of achieving your big life goals?

Will it serve you to present yourself as humble or as a self-promoter? Are you more likely to get there if you live in full take-charge mode or if you invite collaboration, cooperation, and compromise? Should you strive to stand out or to blend in?

Study the people who already have what you want. Can you identify their personal brands? What do they always do that you don't? Is that something you believe you could comfortably adopt and consistently pull off?

Fashion your personal brand in a way that will lead you in the direction you want to go. You can do that only if you absolutely know where you want to go.

3. Consider the Downside

Not to be a bummer, but sometimes we don't really know what we want until we understand what we don't want.

There's no harder sales job than trying to convince others that you are someone you are not. And I dare to guess, there would be no harder life than one you live pretending to be something/someone other than yourself.

Planning a personal brand is a great way to clarify what you truly want and what you believe you're actually suited for. It's an exercise in reflection, research, and reality. It's a way to solidify who you are, what you want, and how to get there.

And it will reveal to you if the brand you think you want really suits you.

PROS AND CONS

Make a list of the pros and cons of the brand you are considering. This could help you realize that you don't have what it takes to behave the way you need to in order to achieve a goal.

If, for example, you want to brand yourself as the next Amanda Gorman—the poised and articulate young poet who brings audiences to their feet—do you believe you can uphold a brand that requires you to speak to large audiences, publicly share your most personal thoughts and creative work, speak your opinion and your mind, and work nonstop on your journey to that post?

Or would you be more comfortable branding yourself as a writer who is published in books, reads poetry at small bookstore gatherings, and confines your political opinions to dinners with friends?

Or perhaps a core value of "service" leads you to plan a personal brand showcasing your devotion to social justice and charity work, but your core value of "independence" requires you to earn more money than a life of volunteering would bring in.

Yes, sometimes our values compete with each other. The best time to discover that is during the planning phase of your personal branding journey—before you start selling yourself as someone/something you cannot sustain.

4. Know Your Triggers

One of the most useful exercises you can do when planning your personal brand is to identify the situations and types of people who push your buttons and tempt you to behave and speak in a way that's off brand.

My friend Sierra has a sharp wit and a sharper tongue. She's impatient and often intolerant when others fall short of her expectations.

She took a job as a project manager at a think tank that staffs up with college interns rather than professionals, so her team consists of a group of bright but inexperienced 20-year-olds. She was excited to be a mentor and work with optimistic young people bursting with energy and ideas.

The brand she planned for herself included words like "mentor" and "teacher." When she made her pros-and-cons list as she considered whether to accept the job, she acknowledged her impatience and high expectations, and she vowed to make "patience" and "flexible" part of her personal brand.

And for the most part, she's knocking it out of the park.

Still, one thing she can't tolerate is people who don't follow instructions. She spends valuable time explaining what she wants. She gets buy-in from her young staff on the best way to complete projects. She makes herself available to answer questions and to help out anyone who needs it, especially someone new to the team.

But when an intern hands in an unfinished project and says it's finished, she raises her voice, displays her impatience, and criticizes that intern a little too harshly and a little too publicly.

She was so tough on one intern that he quit in his third week, even though that meant he would forfeit the college credit he was due for the internship.

Sierra really wants to be a patient person, but that doesn't come naturally to her. But she is determined to get there, with the help of her brand—and a good engagement coach. She even invited the interns to point out when she was acting impatiently. She uses an old-school tactic for changing bad behaviors: She wears a rubber band around her wrist to snap when she catches herself acting that way.

Sierra isn't living her brand perfectly, but she's working toward it—a goal she would not have if she hadn't taken the time to do brand planning and identify triggers that can take her off brand.

Identify your triggers and plan safeguards like Sierra did so you can recognize your off-brand behavior the moment it happens—and eventually stop it before it does.

5. Focus Your Brand on What's Important

You have unlimited choices when it comes to creating a personal brand. You can find lists of hundreds of virtues and values. You could come up with dozens of qualities and characteristics you admire and want to emulate.

I love the saying, "You can't be all things to all people." So be true to yourself and your most important goals.

Narrow your brand down to what is important and realistic, and what will be effective in getting you to where you want to go. Do a few things well rather than trying to do everything at once.

You can always revisit your brand as your needs and goals change over the years. In fact, your brand should evolve throughout your life, just as you do.

But start with what is most important, and live it. You will sell what you live, not what you list.

WHAT ARE YOUR SUPERPOWERS?

A strong and successful personal brand will set you apart from everyone else. So when you plan your brand, take some time to consider which qualities you have that you believe are unique.

What can you do better than the people whom you work with, even your boss? What do your friends always call you for instead of calling someone else? What do you feel you're really, really good at—something you notice that others really don't have?

Those are your superpowers.

Employers hire people with superpowers. They hire people who have hard-to-find skills. They hire people who are natural leaders. They hire people who are good at being part of a team, sharing, negotiating, and keeping the peace.

Not everybody can do those things. What can you do that most others can't?

Need help identifying your superpowers? Pay attention to what others say about you. Do they comment that you always say the right thing? That you're good with children? That you have a way with words? That you always look perfect for the occasion?

Your superpowers are like your signature: They are unique to you. Everybody recognizes them as yours. Everybody can identify them by sight.

Just look at Elon Musk, the gazillionaire cofounder of Tesla and other companies. He knows what his superpower is, and so do you: disruptive technology (like electric vehicles and space travel for non-astronauts). His brand has lots of other facets. He's a father, for example, but his main public focus is on disruptive technology, and look how successful he is.

What is your superpower? Or superpowers?

What does everybody know about you? Equally important: What do you want everybody to know about you? What do you want people to know they can count on your for? What can you live very, very consistently? What is your signature?

I strive for my signature to be kindness. I'm known professionally as the "First Lady of Sales." But my true superpower is the kind way I treat others.

It's my brand promise.

Your personal brand promise is similar to the "promise" a manufacturer makes to you when it builds a product and sells it to you. The manufacturer guarantees that the product will operate properly and that it will serve you as advertised. If it doesn't, you can return it, or you can call an 800 number to complain about it.

When your "product"—you—doesn't live up to your brand, you disappoint your "customers"—the people who bought into your brand—too.

If you intend to use your brand to differentiate yourself from so many other people with the same education and experience as you have, you need to identify the superpower that makes you stand apart from the crowd. And then you need to display that superpower constantly and consistently.

You can't just say you have a superpower. You have to use it like a superhero.

DO YOUR SKILLS MATCH YOUR BRAND?

Once you plan and create your personal brand, the next step is to own it and live it. Are you qualified to do that?

If you choose a brand that you can't live up to, nobody will buy it. That can damage your credibility.

If you brand yourself as a web designer, do you have the skills you need to design really good web pages? Or do you need to take some classes and do a few side jobs before you present yourself as an expert?

If you brand yourself as a fitness influencer, have you learned enough about physiology, nutrition, and exercise science to safely advise your followers about diet and exercise? Or do you need to familiarize yourself with the research or even study for a certification in that area?

Just because you like to do something or would like to be seen as the go-to person for advice on a particular topic doesn't mean you're qualified to do that. It also doesn't mean you can't get qualified. So get qualified to do what you are promising you can do—before you sell a brand that you can't live up to.

My friend told me about her neighbor who loves to sing. She has branded herself as a wedding singer. She tried to get an agent but wasn't able to land one, so she gets her gigs through word of mouth, and mostly from family. She sings at weddings and funerals for a small fee.

My friend tells she me has heard this woman sing at three church events over the past five years or so. Each time, she struggled. Her range is limited, and she has trouble with high notes, which are a staple of church music. Her voice sometimes cracks, and her volume is very low.

She has branded herself as a singer and has sold herself as a singer. She tells people she can sing. She lists the weddings and funerals where she has performed. So people hire her, and then they're surprised when they hear her.

On each of those three occasions, my friend overheard the singer tell people she had a cold or a sore throat that day, and that's why her singing might have been off.

So my friend believes the singer realizes she doesn't sing well, or she wouldn't have felt she needed to make an excuse. My friend doubts the credibility of a singer who doesn't seem to be as talented as her brand makes her out to be.

Here's my point: This woman loves to sing, but she doesn't quite have what she needs to live up to her brand and succeed. If she wants "singer" to be her brand, she could acquire the skills to make her a good singer by taking voice lessons, for example.

I'm totally in favor of branding yourself for the job you want next. Once you do, however, take an inventory of your skills. Then fill in any blanks with lessons or by practicing until you can live up to what you're trying to sell.

Make sure what you're selling is credible.

Do what you need to do to match your abilities to your ambitions. That will make your brand easier to sell.

FIVE MUSTS FOR EVERY PERSONAL BRAND

Here are five solid suggestions for choosing your brand.

1. Choose a Brand That's Authentic

If you would like to present yourself as a dynamo but you're excessively introverted, you won't be able to pull that off. It will be too hard for you to consistently behave in a way that doesn't come naturally to you, if at all.

I've mentioned that a big part of my own personal brand is kindness. So I can't snap at people or make snarky remarks; I can't roll my eyes at others whose views differ from mine. Instead, I have to be a good listener, think before I react, and simply be nice to other people.

This isn't a stretch for me. I grew up in the South, where I was raised to be nice. My whole life, I've tried to be nice to everyone—even to those with whom I disagree or don't care for. I like it when others are nice to me. My philosophy is that nice begets nice; that is, the nicer I am to someone, the nicer he or she will be to me.

This brand works for me because it's already part of my personality.

I'm not saying I don't have moments when I'd rather bite someone's head off than smile, but I try to smile anyway. It's my default. It's how I'm used to acting and reacting. And it's what I have to do to protect my brand. It's what I want for myself.

In short, it's my best version of me. My brand reflects my authentic self.

2. Choose a Brand That Says, "I'm Successful"

Maybe you're not at the top of your field yet. Maybe you don't even have a job yet in that field. Your brand should say you're already there.

You might be young and new to the workplace, and you might like to dress in comfortable T-shirts, jeans, and sneakers for work. That might even be perfectly acceptable where you work. But is that how people dress for the next role you want or the job you hope to land?

Look at the managers, the president of the company, and the members of the board of directors. Do they wear cool kicks to work? Or do they wear a jacket and dress shirt every day and walk around in polished leather shoes?

You can't establish a brand as a successful businessperson if you don't dress like a successful businessperson.

It's true that some very successful entrepreneurs, like Facebook's Mark Zuckerberg, whose daily uniform is a heather-gray T-shirt and nice jeans, have become gazillionaires despite their fondness for casual attire. But when Zuckerberg wanted to be taken seriously during his testimony about Facebook's data privacy and security policies in a congressional hearing, he dressed himself in a suit and tie.

That was a strategic move. It was a part of his plan. He knew his audience. He wanted those congressmembers to see him as a respected businessman.

For us mere mortals, we need to be diligent about looking like what we want to be. When I was a college professor at the beginning of my career, I had a semicasual wardrobe of comfortable dress slacks and twinsets or pullover sweaters, for example.

But when I accepted my first job as a sales consultant and knew I would be meeting with high-level corporate clients, I went shopping for dresses, pantsuits, and nice pumps.

I planned to present myself in an entirely different light to my new colleagues, clients, and supervisors. I made a plan for what I would wear to work.

It's why we dress up for job interviews: We want to look the part. If your goal is to advance to a higher position at work than the one you have now, make dressing for success part of your brand. Dress like you belong in the job you want. Look like the boss you want to be. No matter how casual your workplace is, dressing for success hasn't gone out of style.

3. Choose a Brand That Will Sell Your Message

I work in the sales field, so believe me when I say that your personal brand is the thing that will sell you to potential employers; bosses and teammates at work; and those who are in a position to write letters of recommendation for you or refer you and your company to their colleagues.

My brand, in part, is compassion. I hope that clients want to work with me because they like me. They know I'll be nice to them. They know I'll treat them with courtesy. They know from my behavior and actions that I care about them.

So when they have to choose a consultant to work with, I hope they take my compassion—my brand—into consideration. Same goes when they have to choose a company to hire or refer a colleague to a consultant.

Pin down what you want, and then choose a brand that will get you what you want. Make a plan that will serve as a road map for getting what you want. Make a plan that will help you sell yourself.

Do you want to be discovered so you can have a career in music or acting? Build your brand around that. Plan to be the musician with a catalog of YouTube videos showcasing your talent. Plan to contact every talent agent who represents newcomers and send each of them links to your YouTube performances. Plan to create a social media presence that shows your knowledge, experience, and talent.

A few years ago, my first book, *Every Job Is a Sales Job,* came out. Part of my brand now is "author." To get the book's name out there—and mine—I wrote a plan. I want publishers to know about me so they will ask me to write future books.

So I started by creating a website, DrCindy.com, to promote my book. I sent out emails and wrote articles about the topics my book covers and got them published in business magazines.

All of this is part of my "author/speaker" brand.

Don't simply hope to be discovered. Instead, be proactive. Put your brand out there. Create a brand that gets you discovered. Create a brand that you can sell to those who might discover you.

4. Choose a Brand That Will Position You to Help Others

Branding is all about selling yourself, so figure out how to use your brand as a personal sales tool. One thing I know for sure is that people are more likely to buy what you're selling if there's something in it for them.

My "nice" brand is an example of this. People are more likely to buy what I'm selling because they know I'll treat them right.

Selling yourself is no different from selling products or services. You can spend all day talking about how great your product is, but you're never going to sell it if the buyer doesn't see the value in it. What value do people see in you? Your brand should make that obvious.

Do you present yourself as someone who can help others solve their problems? Advance in their careers? Dress nicer? Save money? Be more popular?

Your brand might seem like it's all about you. But a successful brand shows others that you're a person who can do something for them.

5. Choose a Brand That You Believe You Will Stick With

It's not unheard of for a conservative politician to switch to the other party or to flip-flop on an issue. It's not impossible for a stockbroker to become a cooking and decorating maven (Martha Stewart) or for a figure skater to switch to fashion design (Vera Wang).

But making a total 180 means, for most of us, pretty much starting over with our branding. And that means undoing the brand you already have and creating a new one to match the new you. That can take a considerable amount of time and effort.

So as you choose your brand now, carefully consider if this is what you want for the long haul. In today's media age, branding involves a significant investment of time—and perhaps even money—in creating and curating a social media presence, developing a style or a look for yourself and your media, and steeping yourself in the language, trends, history, and background of the world you're building your brand around.

WRITE IT DOWN

The best way to remember what your brand is and to stick to it is to write your brand words down.

Think of your brand as part of your to-do list for each day. When you write your list of tasks for the day, add your brand buzzwords, like "Be nice" or "Practice patience." Then do it and cross it off your list.

Having your brand words in front of you will help you live your brand every day. Write them on tomorrow's list, too.

Putting your brand in writing will force you to choose specific words that align with specific values and goals. Keeping that paper in front of you will remind you that this is who you want to be and how you want to act.

Sentences, Phrases, and Words

You can format your personal brand any way you want to. Some examples:

- I am a reliable friend and employee. I treat others with respect. I don't just offer help; I figure out ways to be helpful. I put relationships above money, career, and all else.
- I am a future politician. I am an expert on the issues affecting those who live in my state. I am a problem solver. I look and act professional every time I leave my house. I act like I already have the job. I am friendly and take a genuine interest in the concerns of others.

How would you write your brand in a sentence, phrase, or word?

I am a ________________.

I'm an expert in ________________.

My superpowers are ________________.

I always ________________.

I never ________________.

A personal brand is more than a list of words, of course, but compiling such a list will help guide your behavior and remind you to stay on brand. For example:

- Reliable, respectful, helpful
- Political, ambitious, knowledgeable, friendly, interested in others

The more specifically you describe your brand, the clearer you will understand it and the better you can live it.

Write it down. Keep it in your sight. Remember it. Live it.

PART TWO

Live Your Brand

Your beliefs become your thoughts.
Your thoughts become your words.
Your words become your actions.
Your actions become your habits.
Your habits become your values.
Your values become your destiny.

—MAHATMA GANDHI

I love this quote. What a perfect description of personal branding.

Living out your personal brand does not happen automatically. You have to practice it. You have to make it a habit. It has to become automatic for you to recall it whenever you're in a situation that demands it.

If you don't remember your brand, you won't live it. If you don't live it, you can't sell it. If you can't sell it, you can't sell yourself.

Experts say it takes at least 21 days to form a habit. So here's a challenge for you: Every day for the next 21 days—or for however long it takes—practice exercising at least one component of your personal brand. Just one. Do it every day until it's a habit, until it comes naturally, until you wouldn't think of *not* doing it.

If your brand includes "polished and professional," dress up for work every day that you will see anyone, either in person or via camera during a virtual meeting. Wear a professional outfit. Comb your hair. Trim your beard or apply your makeup. Speak up during meetings, with authority. Don't gossip. Don't point fingers. Be accountable. Be on time.

Every day.

If part of your brand is "nice," be conscious about it. Do something nice and unexpected for someone every day. Treat everyone you speak to with kindness. Deliberately do not make snarky remarks, even as a whisper to the trusted colleague sitting next to you, even if it's witty or deserved. Monitor your emails and texts before you send them so you won't send anything that's off brand for you. Be nice.

Once you take the time for this practice, that part of your brand will be a well-known part of you. It will be a habit. It will be what people think of when they think of you.

Once you settle on a brand, act the part, no matter what, at least around colleagues and strangers. Remember: Consistency solidifies your brand. And nothing causes Instagram Stories to go viral quicker than someone who gets caught stepping outside of her self-proclaimed brand.

It's not always easy to stick to your brand, especially when you're tired, you're super busy, you're around colleagues or clients you've gotten to know pretty well, or you're traveling or celebrating.

Sometimes you just want to do what you want to do. Sometimes you feel like saying, "To hell with my brand," just for today. It's like a diet. Some days, you just need a break. But when you indulge, you don't lose weight. And if you blow it off for one day, there's a chance that you'll ditch it for good.

If you don't believe me that the consequences of blowing off your personal brand, even for one day, can be severe, here's a cautionary tale.

The social media influencer Yovana Mendoza Ayres built a personal brand—and earned herself 1.3 million YouTube followers—as Rawvana, a vegan. She shared recipes for raw, vegan breakfast drinks and meals, and once even went on a 25-day water fast. She bragged about how good she felt and showed off her trim, fit body as she filmed her segments wearing short-shorts and midriff-baring tank tops. She preached the importance of "reveal[ing] your authentic self" and urged followers to eat only fruits and vegetables.

That was before another vlogger ran into her at a restaurant and shot and posted a video of the social media star noshing on a plate of fish. The backlash began immediately: One-time devotees shifted into full-on hate mode, calling her a "liar" and a "fake." They called her "Fishvana" and worse.

She explained her fish feast away as the remedy to a health problem she was having. But the damage was done. Her brand was tarnished beyond recovery. She shut down her social media sites and disappeared from the public eye for four months before starting a new site—Yovana—to promote a healthy lifestyle, but not veganism.

The good news for her was that two months in, her new brand had attracted nearly half a million YouTube subscribers, although a fair number continued to post critical remarks.

You may not aspire to be a social media influencer, but your brand is still important for your own reputation. It will definitely suffer if you are ever photographed or videotaped losing control in public.

Your brand should include a commitment to constantly monitor yourself. That might mean that you're thoughtful about what you say, that you think before you speak. It also might mean that you don't party with clients or colleagues, talk behind others' backs, share secrets that we ordinarily would keep private, or behave in a way that some might see as too casual for business acquaintances to be with each other.

Damaging your brand damages your reputation. Bad reputations lead to missed opportunities, lost jobs, angry coworkers, hurt feelings, and shame.

Commit to your personal brand. Sustain your brand. If you can't, then you may have chosen the wrong way to brand yourself.

THE WHOLE PACKAGE

In this ultra-casual world—made even more casual by the stay-at-home culture we have embraced since the pandemic locked us down for so long—I'm the one who likes to show up in business clothes with a full face of makeup and carefully styled hair at every 8 a.m. Zoom meeting.

I've seen people whose brands were "professional, polished, serious, and respectful" show up for virtual meetings wearing their pajamas. I've met with clients whose superpower seemed to be that I could set my clock by them—always on time, prepared to present, and finished on time—straggle into meetings 10 or 15 minutes late when a screenful of folks had gotten up early to meet with them.

I've also received way too many emails from perfectly articulate people but without any capitalized words, with my name misspelled, and with poor grammar and punctuation. That's all part of the impression those people are making. I'll say it again: If you want to sell your brand, you have to live your brand. Not sometimes. Not partway. The whole package—every time you interact with people.

My obsession with always presenting myself according to my brand of professionalism is based on my belief that people view each other as a package deal.

You've heard people refer to someone as "the whole package," right? Maybe it's a groom on his wedding day, when guests are commenting on what a "catch" he is: well employed, good-looking, all-around nice guy. The whole package.

If he were well employed and good-looking but acted like a big jerk, they wouldn't see him as the whole package. If he were a nice guy but couldn't hold down a job, he wouldn't be the whole package in their eyes.

If I brought my coaching expertise and my business savvy and my communication skills to those early morning Zoom calls, but looked like I had to drag myself out of bed to get there, I wouldn't be presenting my whole package to the others on the call.

In fact, if my appearance were any different from how these people experienced me in person, I wouldn't meet their expectation that I not only act professional, but look professional as well. As a result, they might question my professionalism. They might decide my brand for me. I never give them the chance. I want to control my own message and my own brand.

This brand package—your whole package—is based on the five senses. Sales professionals know that the more senses they can appeal to when they're trying to sell you something, the more likely you are to buy it.

Consider how others will perceive you through their five senses: sight, smell, touch, hearing, and taste.

Sight

I know that how I look when I meet people is going to factor into the impression I make on them. So I try to appeal to their sense of sight by trying to look my best whenever I set foot outside my home.

Sure, I dress down on weekends when all I'm doing is running errands and taking walks. But I don't do either of those things in my pajamas. I wouldn't. What if I ran into a client? What if I met a stranger who might be interested in hiring me or striking up a friendship? I cut my odds if I look like a mess. So I always try to look presentable.

Consider how others will perceive you both inside and outside the office, and make sure your appearance is never off-putting.

Smell

Do you wear too much perfume? Do your clothes smell like cigarette smoke? Does your breath smell like your lunch?

Don't let how you smell be what others remember about their first impression of you. Don't let how you smell become an unintentional part of the brand you sell.

Touch

I'm a hugger. I like to give hugs, and I like to get them. But I never touch anyone before I read the room and read the body language of the person I want to hug.

People are touchy about being touched. Some are like big, cuddly teddy bears who make you warm and happy when you embrace them. They hug back.

But others stiffen with discomfort and stand with their arms at their sides if you hug without permission.

Don't touch anyone without asking first or getting a clear nonverbal yes—like if the other person opens his arms to welcome a hug. Don't shake hands without making sure the other person feels safe and healthy doing that. Don't pat someone on the back. Don't pinch anyone for not wearing green on St. Patrick's Day. Don't give a playful punch on the arm.

Our culture has changed over the past few years, and now touching is not OK without consent—even a friendly, nonsexual "attaboy" kind of tap that used to be a normal part of an interaction between colleagues or acquaintances. Others might not be comfortable even shaking hands because of health concerns that started during the pandemic.

That doesn't mean you can't touch—something a hugger like me won't easily abandon. It does mean that you need to read the other person to gauge whether touching is welcome. It means you should verbally confirm that touching is welcome before you touch.

And I wish this went without saying, but it doesn't: Never, ever kiss someone or hug or touch in a way that could be construed as sexual in any way, shape, or form without verbally asking for consent first. Don't do it in the workplace. Don't do it with your friends. And be aware that some of the people you interact with may come from cultures that do not permit touching—or may expect it in certain situations.

A touchy-feely person never made a good first impression, even before #metoo raised public awareness about harassment, boundaries, and appropriateness. Now such a person won't get a chance to make a second impression.

Beware of the damage that unsolicited touching can do to your brand. It can make others uncomfortable around you. It can give the impression that you don't respect the other person or understand the concept of personal boundaries. It can make you seem creepy. Think about a time when someone put an arm around you as a friendly gesture, but it made you uncomfortable. Don't do that to others, even innocently.

Don't make "can't keep my hands to myself" part of your brand. You might never be able to live that down.

Hearing

Do you talk too loudly? Do you mumble so others constantly have to ask you to repeat yourself? Do you hum all day long? Do you chomp on chewing gum, drum your fingers on your desk, have private phone conversations with your speaker on so the people near you in line at Starbucks can overhear every word? Do you gossip with your neighbors or coworkers every chance you get?

That's your brand. That's what people say about you when you're not around. That's the thing people remember about you instead of remembering your superpower.

I laughed when a friend described her next-door neighbors to me. She said the parents yell at each other and at their four children. The children yell at each other and at their dog. Her neighbors yell all day long. They yell when they're outside. They yell so loudly when they're inside that my friend can hear them in her house.

I asked my friend what the family's name was. "I don't know," she said. "We call them the Loudlys."

Another friend has such a mousy voice that it indicates she doesn't have any confidence in what she's saying. On the other hand, I've also heard many people speak to others with such a superior tone that they come off as snobby.

Among them are great leaders, writers, sales reps, teachers, and parents. But that's not what people think about when they run into them at a party or convention. They think "loud," "mousy," "Oh no, here comes that lady who mumbles," or maybe "Oh no! Be prepared to be talked down to."

Have you ever stayed at a hotel near a train track or airport? The noise might have kept you up at night. It might have annoyed you while you were watching TV. It might have distracted you while you were working.

You never stayed at that hotel again, did you?

Listen to yourself. A voice that's too loud or too low is a problem you can fix. Ask your friends for feedback on the "noise" you make before that noise breaks your brand.

Taste

The easiest way to explain how taste affects your brand is to look at a product that tasted so bad it threatened to ruin its company's brand.

An example: New Coke. In an effort to compete better against Pepsi, which is sweeter than Coke, the Coca-Cola Company reformulated its recipe for Coke in 1985, calling it "New Coke." The public didn't like it. Three months later, Coca-Cola brought back its original recipe and rebranded it "Coca-Cola Classic." New Coke hung around until 2002, when the company discontinued it.

People associate experiences and even other people with their sense of taste. For example, when I was in high school, a friend and I were at dinner and she told me she had never tried cheesecake, so I encouraged her to order a slice. She was reluctant because she expected it to taste like cheese but was delighted by the sweet, creamy texture. We're still in touch, and she always reminds me that I'm the one who introduced her to her favorite dessert.

I have one client who makes such a yummy cup of coffee at her office that I always prefer to meet with her in person rather than on Zoom or over the phone.

But if you've ever felt sick after eating a meal at a restaurant, you know the flip side is true, too. You probably never went back to that restaurant.

Taste also comes into play in your brand in a way that doesn't have to do with the senses. Do people say you have good taste? Do they say you leave a bad taste in their mouths?

....

When you're making a first impression, or any impression, realize that your brand isn't limited to how you behave. Your brand is a package, so you need to look, talk, and smell the part.

HOW DO OTHERS PERCEIVE YOU?

Try this exercise. Choose a trusted friend or family member who will be honest with you, and ask these questions:

How would you describe the impression I make based on:

- **How I look at first sight.** Do I appear well dressed, put together, sloppy, etc.?
- **The way I smell.** Is there anything you notice about my scent, my breath, anything that lingers when I walk away?
- **What you feel.** What reaction do you have when I touch your arm, shake your hand, hug you, etc.?
- **What you hear when you're with me.** Am I too loud or quiet? What about my tone of voice? Is there a noticeable noise that I make when I move?
- **My taste.** Do I have good taste in clothes, accessories, possessions? Do I leave a bad taste in your mouth?

FIVE FINAL TIPS FOR LIVING YOUR BRAND

Ready to start living your brand? Keep the following in mind.

1. Don't Go Off Script

During your planning phase—before you ever reveal your new brand—make a list of potential behaviors that could derail your image, reputation, and brand. Resolve to think about your brand before you act.

Make a plan for responding to any accusations or opinions that might tarnish your brand. For example, you could plan to deal with negativity in private, not on social media. A public scandal is bad publicity that isn't good for anybody's brand.

2. Don't Take Your Brand for Granted

People who get too comfortable with their situations tend to lose sight of the fact that it can all go away in an instant at a time when anything can wind up on social media. This makes the need for brand-consistent behavior, conversations, and posts critical.

I'm recalling a bride at her wedding reception who told me, "Now, that's done," as if getting married were an item on her bucket list that she could cross off and forget about. Over the years, she took it for granted that she would always be married, and she did little to work on her relationship with her husband. She never tried to take an interest in his hobbies, like golfing, and didn't encourage him to join her in hers, like buying antique jewelry and selling it at flea markets. After 10 years, she was stunned when her husband said he wanted to end the marriage.

Her brand was "married," and that was that, as far as she was concerned. She never considered that her marital status would ever change.

The same thing can happen at work. If you've been with the same employer for a long time and have gotten lots of promotions, it's tempting to rest on your laurels—to bask in your success so far and believe that your prior accomplishments will carry you forever.

They won't.

A reputation isn't a permanent thing. It can change if you don't keep it up to date. You need to constantly update your brand to keep yourself relevant and respected.

And as we'll see in Chapter 6, even a temporary "vacation" from your brand, if enough people witness it, can erase all the goodwill those prior accomplishments have earned you. And if that lapse winds up on social media—trust me—enough people will witness it.

It's fine to decompress with trusted friends and family members who would never think of publicizing your offhand remarks or jokes. But don't let your guard down with customers, fans, or colleagues who might betray you in order to gain something—like that job you have your eye on—for themselves.

Earn your brand and your reputation every day. Behave consistently as if one misstep could unravel all your considerable efforts to build to your brand.

3. Don't Get Too Big for Your Britches

If your brand makes you more successful, more popular, or wealthier than you ever expected, that doesn't protect you from backlash if you go off brand.

These are extreme examples, but look at comedian Bill Cosby, for one, and family advocate Josh Duggar, for another.

At age 82, Cosby spent time in prison after being convicted of sex offenses in 2018. Reality TV star Duggar, the oldest of 19 children of TV personalities Jim Bob and Michelle Duggar and the former head of a family values group, was exposed as a client of Ashley Madison, a dating site for married people seeking affairs. He also was convicted on child pornography charges and accused of molesting four of his sisters.

Their brands—wholesome TV dad and family-first crusader—were irreparably destroyed.

4. Revisit Your Brand Plan Often

As our jobs change, as we get older, as our tastes mature, and as we achieve our goals, we can outgrow one brand and start building another.

Don't resist it. Instead, plan for it.

Every six months or so, evaluate your progress. Determine whether you need to update your plan. Examine whether your brand needs expanding or tweaking.

5. Be Grateful

Your success at branding won't be possible without the support of both friends and strangers. Once you're living the life you dreamed of, remember who encouraged, supported, praised, and recommended you. Say "Thank you" often and mean it. Make gratitude part of your brand, no matter what else it includes.

LIVING THE DREAM

If you encounter someone who seems to be "living the dream," chances are good that person is faithfully living his or her personal brand.

Oprah Winfrey is a good example. Her brand as the queen of the afternoon talk show was born not only of her talent as a TV host, but of her genuine desire to use that platform to help other people. To that end, she delivered a consistent message on her syndicated show and now in her podcasts, TV interviews, and streaming appearances.

And you won't find Oprah embroiled in a scandal that appears on the pages of grocery store tabloids. You won't hear her bad-mouth other celebrities. That would be off brand for someone whose brand is "helpful and having a positive influence."

Even if your brand is controversial, living it consistently can lead you to success.

Shock jock Howard Stern is one of the most famous radio personalities ever. Considered by some to be "offensive and perverted," he is a multimillionaire who has successfully brought his controversial brand to radio, books, and even to *America's Got Talent*, where he rebranded himself as a judge for four years. In interviews, Stern has said one of the keys to his success is that no matter which media platform he goes to, he tries to remain interesting.

My model (Create. Live. Sell.) of personal branding doesn't include judgment. People who consistently live their personal brands—even those whom you might consider jerks or bigots—often find success because their message is clear and appeals to others who agree with them.

If they presented themselves as different people to different groups, they would unintentionally create the brand of "wishy-washy," "without conviction," or even "sellout."

You'll read in Chapter 6 that this can happen to anyone who picks and chooses when to live the brand and when to go off brand, especially if the off-brand incident is public. And you'll learn that going off brand, especially if you do it often or randomly, can negate the hard work you put into planning your brand.

Live it or nobody will believe it. Live it or nobody will buy it.

If nobody is buying your brand, how will you be able to sell yourself to get what you want?

FINISHING TOUCHES

No matter how often or well you have thought about your personal brand, you won't be ready to sell it until you polish it and practice living it. There are three things you'll need to do:

1. Hold Off on Introducing Your New Brand Until Your Plan Is Solid

In other words, be prepared for your unveiling, just as a company would be before introducing a new product under its brand name.

When you're attempting to brand yourself, you don't want to guess what will stick by trying out one brand after another. Instead, you have to figure out what you'll need to present yourself in this new, branded light—like the right wardrobe, new web pages, and YouTube videos. If you're a mom adding "delegator" to your brand, take some time to teach your older children how to do the chores you're going to stop doing for them. Practice the new behaviors you'll be using as the newly branded you.

Instead of just guessing what will work best for you as you create your personal brand, make a solid plan for what you know is going to work—before you introduce your brand.

For example, someone who hopes to make it as a social media influencer wouldn't post her first video without first arranging a room in her house so it looks good on video or without buying a ring light and a tripod for her camera.

It's important to prepare for your brand's unveiling by having all your props in place before the big day.

That's not to say you can't or shouldn't make small changes to move yourself in the direction of the newly branded you before your grand unveiling. If your aim is to become a YouTube influencer who does clothing hauls and dishes out advice about fashion and beauty, for example, it's a good idea to make it a habit to apply your makeup and press your clothes before you leave the house—even if you're just making a grocery run. Get used to living that way before you announce to the world that this is who you are.

Likewise, if your brand will be that of a successful entrepreneur, go ahead and start talking about your business now so people will believe you know your stuff when you launch your website and seek out speaking engagements. Your brand reveal shouldn't really come as a surprise to anyone. It should not be a total 180 from what the people you work with and socialize with already expect from you. But it should coincide with a persona that is more focused, more consistent, and more public than before.

2. Write Down the Details

If you're new to branding, you might be surprised that the people with the strongest brands have choreographed everything about their public selves—from the way they walk, to the clothes they wear, to the catchphrases they speak. Celebrities plan which restaurants they will be seen in, whom they will be seen with, and what they will say in case a fan or media reporter approaches them.

Most of us don't have to be that precise, of course. But I can tell you that I plan my outfits for the days when I will meet clients, potential clients, the public, or my own team. I plan how much sleep I need to get so I'll look fresh and be on my game when I travel. I plan how I will introduce myself, how much of my personal story I will reveal to strangers, and how much time I will devote to fixing my hair and applying my makeup. I don't want to be stranded—and by that I mean unprepared—because I haven't planned for the things that are important to uphold my brand.

This paid off big-time when I wound up sitting on an airplane right across from the CEO of a company that was on my list of potential clients. Thank goodness I wasn't in my yoga pants; I would never dress that way for a business trip. That would not be on brand for me. The CEO and I wound up sharing a cab after the flight, and sure enough, he became my client.

I can't remember everything I need to do without writing it down. Neither can you. Write your plan down in intricate detail.

Someone who wants to brand himself as a thought leader, for example, could make a list of the philosophies he wants to push. He could write down the causes he wants to publicly embrace. That will help him get used to steering conversations in the direction of the topics he wants to associate himself with.

In my first book, *Every Job Is a Sales Job*, I introduced Ben, one of my favorite contractors. Ben works for a company that has started asking homeowners to fill out a customer satisfaction survey every time one of its employees visits their home. Ben has decided he wants to get more positive survey results than any of his coworkers and brand himself as the guy who wins Employee of the Month honors the most months in a row.

Ben does not leave this to chance. Every time he arrives at a home, he covers his shoes with cloth booties so the homeowner can see that he cares about not making a mess. He engages in a few minutes of friendly small talk before he starts working. He uses his considerable skills to resolve the problem the homeowner has described. He asks what else he can do while he's there, even if the extra job wasn't on the original work order.

He asks each customer if he has done satisfactory work. He asks each homeowner if he has behaved respectfully. He asks each homeowner to ask for him by name next time. He hands each homeowner his business card, which he had printed himself because the company does not supply those.

Finally, he hands the homeowners the survey and asks if he should wait while they fill it out. He knows that the more surveys his customers fill out, the better his chances of becoming Employee of the Month.

Ben made a plan for how to approach each homeowner. He wrote a checklist of activities and questions. He ordered business cards. He set his strategy.

Ben has always been a hard worker and popular with customers. But what he did yesterday won't earn him stellar survey results today and tomorrow.

Ben is protecting his brand, his reputation, and his future. He never takes it for granted that his past will carry him through.

3. Rehearse

How you look, what you say, and how much confidence you project will determine whether your brand is believable and consistent. So practice all those things before you present yourself in public.

Taking your branded self out for a spin is a little bit like giving a speech. You never go on stage unprepared.

When you create a personal brand, the world is your stage. A fitness coach will kill his brand if he sits at his desk at the gym eating french fries. A young executive will quickly burn his wunderkind reputation if he hangs out until the wee hours drinking with the employees he supervises and starts showing up late to work in the morning.

Plan for all that. Know that you're on stage—and quite literally could show up on somebody's Instagram feed—any time you leave your house. Plan to dress the part. Plan to act the part. Plan how you will say yes and how you will say no to invitations and opportunities that could help or hurt your brand.

The more you plan, the less likely you are to forget who you have decided to be and how you have decided to present yourself. The less likely you will be to slip. The better your brand will be.

And the more ready you will be to start selling it.

5

Living Your Company's Brand

For a brand to be successful and effective, it's important to live it every day. That can be a challenge when you find yourself living it in an environment that regularly throws unexpected challenges in your path, requires you to make decisions quickly, and pushes all the buttons you aim to control by living your brand.

Nowhere is that more pronounced than in the workplace.

Everyone experiences pressure at work, at least some of the time. Bosses make unreasonable demands on your time. Coworkers slack off just when your team's deadline approaches. Office mates grind on your nerves. Your employees behave disrespectfully. The coffeemaker breaks down just as you begin your overtime shift.

If you're truly living your brand, none of that will tempt you to deviate from your best self.

Even during off hours, good employees experience a certain amount of pressure to live up to not only to their own stellar brands, but to the company's brand as well. As an employee, you are a brand ambassador for your employer, even though that may not be part of your job description.

For example, if you get a job at your favorite clothing store and you start wearing that store's clothes all the time, you're letting everyone you meet know that you love what you're selling. If you can't stop talking to friends and family about how much fun you're having with a project at work or how much you like your coworkers, you're plugging your company, which could lead others to apply to work there or to trust that business's products.

But every time you complain about work, make a snarky comment about your boss, or roll your eyes when someone points out a flaw in your company's product, you send a message to the people you're with: My company isn't living up to its brand. That's not OK. More and more, companies rely on their employees not only to create, live, and sell personal brands that are compatible with the company's mission and vision, but to behave as ambassadors of that mission and vision even when they're off the clock.

Part of this new focus on employees' personal brands comes from a shift in consumer behavior. Potential customers are using social media more than ever to learn about products and to check out who else is using them. They want to know what people like them are saying about those products and about the company that makes them. They certainly want to know if celebrities like the Kardashians like the products and the company. And they want to know that the company's own employees stand behind their employers and their employers' brands.

If you're talking smack about your company to the other parents at your kid's soccer game on Saturday, you could be turning off potential customers.

If you include your employer's name on your social media profiles and then post photos of yourself in a way that could be construed as inappropriate, racist, or sexist, you could be giving potential customers the impression that your company endorses your behavior.

Companies know that, too, and some are starting to adopt policies restricting what employees may post on their personal social media. If you identify yourself as an employee of one of these companies, you have to watch what you say about your job, your colleagues, and the business.

Your personal brand and the way you live it—in your social and home life, on social media, and with your coworkers in the workplace—influence your company's ability to live up to its own brand. In short, if people like your personal brand, they tend to like your employer's brand, too.

Not only are some companies encouraging their employees to create, live, and sell personal brands that reflect well on the organization—they are hiring trainers to help the workers achieve that.

I've worked with multiple companies that have asked me to help their employees create personal brands that both the employees and their companies can be proud of.

The companies themselves were going through a rebranding and wanted their employees—all of them, not just the sales staff or the public-facing executives—to rebrand as well. I helped the employees understand how what they do and say, even outside of work, reflects on their employers.

I helped them become ambassadors for their companies.

As we will see in Chapter 6, business owners are swiftly dismissing employees who go off brand in public. They don't keep employees who behave badly in public, especially when those bad acts—however out of character for the employee—are captured on video and posted all over social media or the nightly news.

So when you plan your personal brand, take some time to evaluate how it might reflect on your employer. And if you face an opportunity to go off brand—to have a little fun, to promote a controversial cause, or to take an uncharacteristic action—think first about whether what you're about to do could make you or your employer look bad.

Sure, it takes a bit of the spontaneity out of life. Consistency always does. Living your brand means staying on brand. And staying on brand simply means honoring the tough decisions you made during the thoughtful process of creating your brand in the first place.

MORE THAN AN EMPLOYEE

When I lived in Washington, DC, a few years ago, I had a conversation with a very public-facing broadcaster, Shawn Anderson, who had thoughtfully planned a personal brand that took into account the considerable influence his behavior could have on the reputation of the radio station where he works.

Shawn is the afternoon drive-time anchor for WTOP Radio in Washington, DC, one of the largest, most successful all-news radio stations in the country. He has worked there for more than 25 years, and it's no accident that he has never needed to explain his behavior to his bosses.

That's because he never goes off brand, at least outside of the comfort of his home, family, and closest friends.

When Shawn refers to his personal brand, he calls it "Shawn Anderson." The Shawn Anderson brand is professional. It has a big voice. It's up to date on news, politics, sports, and pop culture. It's friendly to strangers, grateful to listeners, and happy to "hold court" when friends of friends corner him at parties because they're thrilled to meet him and talk with him.

Shawn Anderson is upbeat and alert at all times. He's quick on his feet. He responds to criticism with curiosity and gratitude. He carefully guards his political opinions so nobody who listens to him on the radio will suspect him of bias. He doesn't criticize newsmakers. He limits his contribution to conversations to the facts. He answers, "What do you think?" with the facts he knows about both sides. It's a good conversation, but you'll always walk away without knowing which side he's on.

Shawn refers to Shawn Anderson as "me, plus 10 percent." I love that. It perfectly encapsulates what living your brand means: you, plus 10 percent. Always "on." Always at your best. I've embraced that description as part of my own personal brand: My Dr. Cindy brand is me, plus 10 percent.

When Shawn can't sustain that extra 10 percent, he stays home.

So do I. So should you.

If Shawn feels he's not up to being Shawn Anderson on a Saturday and he's expected at an optional social gathering, he declines the invitation.

When Shawn Anderson shows up, you get Shawn Anderson. He shows up as exactly what you would expect if you listen to him on WTOP: smart, well informed, unbiased, upbeat, happy, and grateful.

Regular Shawn is authentically all those things. But some days, he's just tired. Sometimes he needs a quiet day. Every now and then he needs to chill in front of the TV and watch three football games in a row.

We all need to do that. We need to take care of ourselves. That's what he does on those days. In the process, he protects his brand. He doesn't put himself in a public situation on a day when Shawn Anderson needs to be just Shawn.

You'll get this once you start living your brand, day in and day out. That extra 10 percent can exhaust you, even if you live an authentic, natural brand.

By living the Shawn Anderson brand in public, and by staying out of the public eye on the rare occasions when he doesn't feel he can give that extra 10 percent, Shawn is protecting his company as much as himself.

His fans expect Shawn Anderson when they see him. And his company expects Shawn Anderson to be an ambassador for the radio station.

Work and life are intertwined for all of us, not just for public figures. Our personal brand really isn't just personal. It's a reflection of who we are in the context of what we do for a living.

Follow this stellar example as you practice living your own brand. Commit to it, live it, and protect it—even if that means taking a day off from it, very privately, every now and then.

LIVING YOUR COMPANY'S BRAND

Describe your company's brand in three words.

Imagine a conversation in which you describe your company's brand to someone you just met on an airplane or at a social event.

Is your brand as an employee and/or manager consistent with your company's overall brand?

How can you be a better brand ambassador, both inside your company, with clients and company stakeholders, and with the public?

MANAGERS VERSUS LEADERS

Shawn is a great example of a leader who lives his brand. He's not a manager at work; he's considered "talent." But he's a leader because he sees the big picture, he is influential with the public and his coworkers, and he recognizes the importance of inspiring and motivating those around him.

A manager can be a leader, and a leader can be a manager. But branding yourself as a leader or printing the title on your business card doesn't make you one, especially if you don't truly understand the difference between management and leadership.

To live your "leader" brand, learn that difference: Managers focus on process, and leaders focus on people. Learning the difference will help you, as a manager, sell your brand as a leader while still getting your work done as a manager.

- Leadership is about big ideas and the big picture. Managers focus on right now and next week, but leaders anticipate next year. What is happening now is rarely as important as what's coming next. Leaders don't let the future catch them off guard.
- Leaders inspire innovative thinking even under difficult circumstances. When the pandemic sent employees home to work remotely, managers drilled down to the nuts, bolts, and tactics that employees would need to work effectively. Leaders stepped up to energize and engage their work teams—which at the time included employees who were resistant, depressed, anxious, and grieving—and led by example.
- Good leaders accept that employees are human beings with fears, emotions, and after-hours responsibilities. Goals and objectives, sales charts, strategic plans, and vision statements are all critical to success. But those are built on the capabilities and limitations of human beings. Leaders tap into their employees' value and uniqueness in order to inspire them to do their best work.

Do you brand yourself as a leader but focus more on your role as manager? Even if you are an employee with no "manager" or "leader" title at work, your brand as an informal leader will solidify as you show your great influence on others as a motivator and visionary.

Live your leadership brand every day. It will help you be the best leader you can be, even as you get into the nitty-gritty of your management responsibilities.

MANAGER *MIS*BRANDS

Simply knowing what the role of a manager is won't make you a good one. Sometimes you need to know what *not* to do in order to create, live, and sell your perfect work brand. Here are some common brands that managers don't realize they're selling.

The Barker

Everyone has met one of these. It could be a boss, a parent, a coworker, or even a teenager who volunteers to chair the prom committee at school.

The barker, as they say, "barks" orders. The barker tells you what to do, often without explanation. This manager has a vertical communication style: The orders come from the top down without room for bottom-up feedback or even questions. The barker doesn't consider the feelings of employees and doesn't attempt to get buy-in from the people who do the work, even though they might know a better way to do it than the barker insists upon.

The barker often doesn't know—or perhaps doesn't care about—the impact this kind of dictatorial style has on the people on the receiving end. This manager might feel she has a right to command others to do what she says. She probably believes her brand is "strong, authoritative, in charge."

As you know, however, a brand is only as strong as the perception others have of it. And her employees very likely have branded her as "mean, bossy, harsh, and unfair."

Barking orders is no way to make a sale. Would you ever return to your favorite ice cream parlor if your server barked at you when you placed your order? Part of a manager's job is to clearly communicate what needs to get done, train the employees who will do the work, answer questions from those who need clarity, and motivate the team to do its best. That's how to sell employees on doing what you ask.

The barker's brand certainly is not "good manager" or "good motivator." Her orders often result in half-hearted work or mistakes born of confusion.

If this manager is hoping to sell her employees on doing a good job, she's definitely barking up the wrong tree.

The Best Friend

Bosses, parents, teachers, and others who manage other people sometimes adopt the attitude that the more their teams, children, or students like them, the better they will perform.

That's true to a point. People often respond to an empathetic, collaborative manager by working their best to make him proud. Most people return the respect and trust their manager shows them.

However, good managers balance a healthy give-and-take with employees with a clear boundary that leaves no question about who is in charge. A good leader's brand, no matter how kind and understanding he is to the people who work for him, includes "authority."

That authority fades when a boss goes too far to get his employees to like him. It's hard for a supervisor to maintain an "I'm in charge" brand when he also sells himself as their best friend.

This can happen if you get promoted to team leader over a group you have worked with for a while and know well. It's hard to go from peer to manager when you're used to hanging out with your teammates after work, drinking with them, confiding in them, or even getting into trouble with them.

It's hard to go from buddy to boss—or at least to an effective boss—when the people you now supervise used to be your best friends.

The tendency is to believe you can have both: close friendships with your employees and authority over them. The best-friend manager quickly discovers that he has to sacrifice something: authority or friendship. One of those brands inevitably suffers once the manager has to hold his after-work friends accountable at work.

Getting promoted over the heads of their existing friends isn't the only way managers wind up with the unsustainable brand of best-friend manager. Sometimes they create it deliberately so their employees will like them.

An example: Matt's favorite part of his job as a college professor is the relationships he forges with his students. Matt's teaching style is hands-on and collaborative. He loves to teach a concept or a process, and then work side by side with his students as they complete a project that requires them to use the skills they have learned.

Often that means he works late into the evenings with the students. He springs for pizza if they work past dinnertime. He takes breaks with them. The students bond with each other and with him.

He invites students to call him Matt. He gives them his mobile number so they can call or text him any time with questions about their assignments. He tells them about his weekends with his family. He understands when they have trouble finishing their work on time. In short, he treats them as friends.

Or he used to. One semester, nearly all the students who finished Matt's freshman course enrolled next in the more advanced sophomore section, which he also taught, because they enjoyed the first class so much. A few weeks in, Matt noticed that many of these students stopped meeting their deadlines or studying for quizzes. One even asked him for quiz questions in advance—a request, of course, that he denied.

Another student mentioned to him that the group figured Matt "would be cool" about late and missed assignments.

Matt asked her how they came to believe that.

"You're Matt," the student replied. "You're like our cool uncle. We're friends."

Matt's brand: "friend, fun, cool."

Matt likes it that his students think of him that way. But he believes his brand is much more than that: "responsible adult, supervisor, educator." He has a syllabus to follow and requirements for his students to meet to get course credit.

In fact, he's not at all cool with late or missed assignments—except in an emergency.

But he sold the "cool uncle" brand at the expense of the "professor" brand, and the students bought into the fact that his brand did not include "disciplinarian" or "tough grader."

He sold the wrong thing.

I'm not saying you can't get to know the people you supervise or treat them in a friendly way. But it's rarely possible for a manager to live his brand as an authority figure if he's also trying to brand himself as everyone's best friend.

Not sure which side you fall on? Ask your employees. Like Matt's student, they'll be happy to flatter you with their perception that you're cool. You need to decide, at what cost?

A manager shouldn't be selling friendship; he should be selling trust and respect.

The Pushover

A manager who shies away from conflict probably won't be a manager for long.

I had a client who said yes to everything his employees asked him for: extended deadlines, extra days off, easier assignments.

This client thinks his brand is "casual" and "nice guy." To his team, however, his brand is "pushover."

His employees also have branded him as "wishy-washy" because no matter what objection or exception they ask for after he announces a decision, he'll cater to it. He doesn't defend or explain his decisions; he simply abandons them at the first hint of pushback from the staff.

His employees like him. Why wouldn't they? But they don't respect him. Why would they?

The Memo Maker

Good communication skills are the hallmark of any good manager. Good communication skills include the ability to talk to employees—both one-on-one and as a team.

To avoid suffering from a "pushover" brand, one of my clients promptly responded to every complaint, suggestion, and problem by emailing the full staff a long memo full of double exclamation points and passages highlighted in red. He did this almost daily.

If someone shared a problem involving an assignment or a coworker, this manager wrote a memo about it instead of talking it through with the employee. If an employee messed up and needed coaching or discipline, the manager wrote a memo about it—in general terms, without the employee's name—so the whole staff could benefit from the answer.

The manager believed his brand was "responsive" and "nice guy." His employees, on the other hand, considered him "impersonal" and his memos a joke.

His management style created a lot of unnecessary emergencies because he spent so much time sending emails that he couldn't keep up with the ones he received. Plus his employees stopped reading his memos because they were long and treated every situation as if it were the most important matter of the day. And they didn't feel like the manager had enough time or interest in them to talk to them face-to-face.

That manager's brand created an inefficient work environment. It also ended his career as a manager.

The Fearmonger

Some managers mistake fear for respect, so they raise their voices, make threats, and belittle their employees.

One leader I heard about often says, "They should be afraid of me."

Does fear translate into getting his employees to do what he wants them to do? Absolutely. They're afraid not to. They're also looking for new jobs and, more frequently, complaining about their boss to human resources.

Fear and respect are not the same thing. The fearmonger believes his brand is "respected," but his employees perceive him as cruel. His behavior is breaking their spirits and sapping any sense of loyalty or passion they ever had for their jobs.

This leader doesn't believe his employees will quit, but it's only a matter of time.

The Imposer

One small business owner I know is so passionate about his vision and his work that he can't tolerate any employee who doesn't share it.

Granted, it's affirming when the people who work for you are as committed to your company's success as you are. But most of them probably aren't willing to make as many sacrifices as the person who started the business.

This owner is frustrated when employees can't work on weekends because they have family and social obligations. He once fired a hard worker who refused to work past 3 p.m., even though her shift started at 7 a.m. and she accepted the job, in part, so she would be able to be home in the afternoons with her school-age children.

This owner has branded himself as "passionate, visionary, and committed," and there is no doubt he is all those things. But he expects his employees to alter their brands to suit his—and that's unreasonable.

To them, his brand is "imposing, unreasonable, and unconcerned about us as people."

The Micromanager

Micromanagers sell one thing to their employees: "I don't trust you."

If the only time your employees get to put their ideas into practice is when you're on vacation, you're holding them back.

Micromanagers do their employees' work for them, or do it over because it's never good enough. The micromanager believes her brand is "helpful." Her employees perceive her brand as "control freak."

And they believe their manager does not trust in their competence. She doesn't trust them to get the job done. She doesn't appreciate their talents.

That managerial brand is defeating. It makes employees feel like there's no point in trying because there's no way what they will do is correct. It makes them feel undervalued and even worthless.

When a manager asks for input and feedback and allows employees to spread their wings, on the other hand, she says to the staff: "I hired you because you're smart and talented. I can't wait to see what you do with this project."

....

Just as any employee needs to create and live a personal brand that reflects well on the company, so do managers and leaders.

If someone in a position of authority is living a brand that makes employees feel belittled, undervalued, unproductive, or unhappy, those workers are likely to believe the company supports that position as well.

If you are a manager or leader—or if you aspire to those positions—make yourself a role model for your employees. Create and live a brand that they can respect and even emulate.

All employees, including managers and leaders, need to be ambassadors for the company—and not just with people outside of the company. They need to represent the company's values and mission with their own employees so those workers will feel proud and happy to work there.

6

Off Brand

A middle school teacher lost her job after her preteen students reposted photos of her in a skimpy bikini that she shared on Twitter. A lawyer and a police officer were both dismissed after participating in a political protest. Many others are on a long list of those who did things so contrary to their companies' core values that their employers couldn't keep them around.

Businesses don't want to associate with employees who behave in a way that is unbecoming for whatever field they work in. Their companies know that the reputation of their employees equals the reputation of the business.

The same thing has happened countless times when companies have hired popular celebrities to endorse their products in TV ads and then fired them for making suspect comments on social media or in interviews. Mountain Dew ditched rapper Lil Wayne after a new song included what the company perceived as racist lyrics. Nike parted ways with NFL running back Adrian Peterson after he was indicted for allegedly abusing his son. Actress and comedian Roseanne Barr got kicked off of her own TV show after tweeting racist comments about a senior advisor to then-President Barack Obama. Kevin Hart, also an actor and comedian, resigned from coveted Academy Awards hosting duties after his decade-old tweets with homophobic comments surfaced.

These celebrities sold themselves as funny, talented, and artistic. As they evolved as performers, their brands also evolved, into "popular," "in demand," and "moneymakers."

So when they stepped out of those brands and into words and behavior that seemed out of character, it was shocking to many. It also raised the question, "Who is this person, really?" And it led many sponsors and fans to conclude, "This person's brand is fake."

For their sponsors and employers, it planted some serious doubts. How will this affect the reputation of my business? Will it negatively affect sales? Will employees and potential employees refuse to work here because the business is associated with this person?

The fact is, most businesses aren't willing to wait and find out. Their action is swift, and they rarely defend the off-brand offender.

It only takes one off-brand incident for employers, colleagues, and even some of our friends to question who we are when we do something totally out of character if it is inappropriate.

Think about it. If you sell yourself as nice and then you do something really mean, what are people supposed to think? Are you nice, or are you mean? Was this just a one-off, or have you been faking the nice part all along? Have I been duped? Are you going to be mean again? Are you going to be mean to me?

Talk show host Ellen DeGeneres, for example, had branded herself as nice. But her show ended earlier than she had planned after celebrity guests and her own staff accused her of only being nice for the cameras. Even when her defenders claimed the bad behavior wasn't Ellen's, but her producers' and managers', it was her brand—and her show—that suffered.

Bottom line: Going off brand can ruin your brand. Going off brand can kill your credibility.

Chances are, you'll also lose your job, and your employer is not going to hire you back. And future employers won't want to take a chance in case you'll do the same thing again.

You'll need to work awfully hard to regain the trust of those who bought your brand. But it's not impossible. Kevin Hart is back on the A-list, after all. But it's not easy, especially for those of us who aren't celebrities.

So think before you act. When you're deciding whether to make a bold move, to go off script, to get even with someone, or even to make a snarky remark, ask yourself: "Is this really me?" "Is this going to damage my reputation?" "What is this going to cost me?"

Think about your job. You don't have to be a celebrity spokesperson for a very public incident to have a negative impact on your reputation and the reputation of your company. More and more, businesses are quick to detach from anyone who shows a deep character flaw, even if it was a single, past mistake—and especially if it smells anything like racism, sexual harassment, partisan politics, or illegal behavior.

Many companies are relying on the reputations and personal brands of their employees to make them look good—and they expect employees to stay on brand both on and off the job. Damaging your own reputation is very likely to also damage your company's.

In addition, more and more consumers expect the companies they buy from to have high standards and to reflect their customers' values. As a result, more firms are hiring people based, in part, on how closely job candidates' personal values align with their customers' values.

And they're firing people whose behavior does not reflect those values.

Your brand portrays you at your best. Your social media brand is basically a highlight reel of your life. Your posts show the world what you want it to see. They make your first and lasting impression on anyone who sees them.

But anyone can post anything about you on that highlight reel, which plays 24/7, forever, and that can have a damaging impact not only on your own reputation, but on your employer's.

And don't think for a minute that your employer will not find out what you say and do when you're off the clock. Bad news travels fast. Social media is lightning quick to spread the word—and the video. You simply cannot take anything back in an age when anyone could be recording your every move, even if you didn't give permission or you didn't know you were being recorded.

ALL IS NOT LOST

All of that being said, I can offer some hope to those who have bungled their brands.

My best advice is to follow the tried-and-true process that public relations professionals swear by when the companies or celebrities they work for suddenly find themselves in a crisis or scandal.

Step 1. Make a Plan

This first step will come as no surprise now that you're deep into this book. Planning is always my first step.

Ideally, your plan would be in place before a crisis ever occurs. It's not so much that you need to expect trouble, but you really do need to plan for it, just in case. You need to be ready to defend your brand.

As you create and curate your brand at the start, take some time to consider what could go wrong. Sales professionals do this before every sale. They think about the objections and concerns they may encounter. Ask yourself:

- In what way could the brand I will create, live, and sell rub some people the wrong way?
- Is it possible that any part of my brand—and therefore my intentions—might be misunderstood?
- How could someone use my brand against me?
- What potential circumstances could arise that might throw me off my brand? For example, what might cause me to overreact or to react badly?
- Is there any part of my personality, philosophies, or beliefs that truly is contrary to the brand I intend to sell?

- How easy will it be for me to stick to my brand all the time? Where are my weaknesses in the context of the brand I am going to sell?

Once you consider what could go wrong, you can plan to do three things:

1. Avoid those situations so you can stay on brand.
2. Determine how you will stay on brand with your behavior and reactions should those situations arise.
3. Prepare your response in the unlikely event that you really mess up.

Step 2. Tell the Truth

Don't deny anything that you did. Someone, somewhere has it on video. Or there were witnesses. If you're falsely accused, it's OK to say so. But own the truth. Own your behavior. Don't lie; you'll get caught, and that will make it worse. The lie has a way of becoming a bigger blunder than whatever off-brand behavior you actually engaged in.

Nobody wants to be branded as a liar. And it only takes one lie to get there. Stick with the truth.

It's not easy owning up to a mistake. It's embarrassing. It's even harder when it's an honest mistake or when you really didn't mean any harm. A good plan, of course, will prepare you to catch yourself before you make the mistake. But once you do, it's yours.

Step 3. Say You're Sorry

Sincerely. For real. Not just lip service. Professional business and life coaches often encourage their clients to look for any glimmer of truth in every accusation. Find that. Acknowledge that you understand why what you did upset people or was wrong. Explain what happened and why. Confess that you didn't realize the impact it would have on others. Take an inventory of how you're feeling about hurting or offending people.

Say you're sorry. Do not act defensively.

Apologize to each individual you hurt, if it's just a few. Apologize publicly if what you did has become public. Apologize on social media if need be. Cover your bases. Let everyone know how sorry you are.

And feel sorry; don't just say it. Feel for the people you hurt. Offer to make it right if you can. Take it back if you can.

Step 4. Act Fast

Remember that sketchy thing you did to your sibling/friend/neighbor when you were little and your parents made you apologize to the kid you offended/hurt/stole from/lied about? And do you recall that nobody believed your forced apology actually meant that you were sorry?

That's the reaction you'll get if you delay your apology until someone calls for it. Get ahead of it. Did you do something wrong? Apologize on the spot. How you react in the first few hours after any offense will determine how hard it will be for you to recover from it.

Acting quickly can head off gossip. It can stop people from trying to fill in the blanks with their own invented scenarios about what happened.

The first one to explain what supposedly happened is the one whom the most people will believe. So be the first one.

Know that you're in a race against the speed of social media to get your point of view out there before others have the chance to skew the facts or convince any listener that their opinion and not yours is the official viewpoint.

Step 5. Learn from Your Mistake, and Do Better Next Time

Make it clear to anyone who was affected that the incident taught you something and that you won't repeat your mistake.

When you step so far out of your brand that people can barely believe what you did or said, you have a small window to convince them that they're right. It wasn't your usual, controlled self. It wasn't like you. Here's what happened. You're sorry. It won't happen again.

This, like any opportunity to persuade others, is a sales job. You need to sell others—your boss, your friends, your family, your social media followers—that your brand is solid and your lapse was a one-time thing. If it wasn't, you need to sell others on trusting you to learn and grow from the experience.

And then you need to get right back on brand. And make a better plan to stick with it.

BRANDING BLUNDERS

In Chapter 2, we met Bikini Girl, whose split-personality brand was standing in the way of her success either as a model or as a documentary filmmaker.

But the split-personality brand is far from the only branding blunder.

Those who commit these blunders often don't realize that the brand they think they are selling is not the one that other people are buying.

For example, do you have a colleague who is a big jerk? Unfortunately, many people do!

Is your colleague selfish, thoughtless, loud, bossy, and offensive? Do people talk about him and say they don't like him?

It's unlikely that he carefully curated the brand of "selfish and offensive." But that's his brand, whether he knows it or not.

The thing is, he is who he is. He's probably always on brand. He never deviates, right? He's never thoughtful, giving, demure, or considerate. Never. He never goes off brand.

Even if his brand is awful, it's his. He owns it. He lives it. He sells it.

Not everybody does.

Too often, we believe we live and sell the brand we so carefully created, and we don't realize that we're unintentionally selling something else.

Here is a sample of what can go wrong without your permission.

The Saboteur

Sometimes others identify us with something quirky that we say or do over and over, even though it has no impact on our quality or qualifications. And that quirk becomes what we sell—instead of our quality or qualifications.

An example: In the 15 years since she got her master's degree in biology, Margaret has carved out a successful career as a researcher. People know she's smart and experienced.

Yet when the lead researcher interrupts her to ask for a status report, her answer, invariably, is, "I'm sorry." In staff meetings, before she asks for clarification of an assignment or a colleague's concept, she says, "I'm sorry." After she gets the explanation, she says, "I'm sorry," again.

She's sorry she wasn't quicker to look up from her microscope, even though she wasn't expecting a visit from the lead researcher. She's sorry she needs clarification, even if the colleague's presentation was full of holes. She's sorry that she asks so many questions. She's sorry that she believes she found the answer when nobody else could.

Or is she?

She thinks her personal brand is "well educated, highly qualified, deeply experienced." Everyone around her thinks her brand is "the one who says, 'I'm sorry' all the time."

That's how her colleagues identify her. That's what they joke about behind her back. Some of them even call her "I'm sorry" instead of "Margaret."

What do you do by habit, instinct, or fear that people associate you with? Do you have a catchphrase that isn't doing you or your brand any favors? Are you selling people on the fact that you're sorry rather than on the fact that you're capable and worthwhile? Is your brand making you the brunt of a joke? Are you wearing gigantic purple glasses and unaware that everyone calls you "purple glasses lady" instead of "awesome graphic designer?" Do you ask people, "What would your cat do in this situation" as a joke—without realizing that you, in their eyes, *are the joke*?

Tip: Listen to yourself when you talk. Observe your own behavior. What are you doing or saying that has become, to others, who you are? And what is that association stealing from you? How is it branding you in a way that's opposite of a brand based on your accomplishments and your contributions?

Don't expect anyone to tell you you're misbranding. They're having too much fun imitating you when you're not around to defend yourself, or to say, "I'm sorry" for saying "I'm sorry" all the time.

Pay attention to yourself. And then stop sabotaging your brand. Stop making that accidental sale over and over again. You're selling the wrong thing.

Blurred Lines

With so many of us working from home, the lines between work and personal lives have become blurrier than ever. Professionals let their cats walk across their keyboards in full view of clients or managers during virtual meetings. Colleagues who, just a couple of years ago, wouldn't set foot out of their homes in the morning without full makeup and business attire are showing up to their half-empty offices wearing sweatpants and uncombed hair. Parents don't think twice about interrupting even important meetings to answer phone calls from their kids. College students tell their professors they have to miss class for a family emergency—which turns out to be a brother who needed a lift to work.

That might be cute or funny or sweet—the first time you do it. If it's consistent, however, it messes with your brand.

If your brand is professional, or reliable, or serious about work, school, or whatever your commitment is, then it's time to draw a thicker line between work and personal business. That's hard to do under the best circumstances, but especially if your home is your office and your office is your home. It can sometimes feel not like you're working from home, but like you're living at work.

Boundaries are key to keeping work and personal life separate. That cuts both ways, though.

First, decide what brand you want to sell at work. Is it casual, carefree—even careless—because you're at home while you're working and meeting with clients? Or is it professional, no matter where you make your calls or participate in virtual meetings?

It can't really be both, at least publicly. If you're not dressing, appearing, and behaving the part of the brand you want to sell, you're selling the wrong thing.

Second, let others know what your boundaries are. Unless you want your brand to be "available 24/7," you'll need to proactively and consistently enforce your boundaries. Don't answer texts or agree to appointments when you have personal time scheduled.

Tip: Selling your brand means living your brand. Too many exceptions to your own rules invite others to assume your brand has changed.

My Mom Made Me

Gianni's dad was an attorney, and so was his grandfather. All his life, his family assumed he would be a lawyer, too. So he went to law school and joined the family firm. He hates it.

Gianni wants to be an architect. He loves drawing and urban planning and old buildings. On vacations, while others are shooting photos of landmarks, Gianni is sketching them. But he's a good son, and he wants to please his parents.

Gianni thinks his brand is "successful lawyer," but to many who realize that he gave up his dream to satisfy his parents, his brand, at age 30, is "obedient child."

More people than you might think are living brands that someone else chose for them. It could be parents, siblings, or even friends. We often try to live up to the expectations of others to the point that we can wake up one day and wonder whose life we're living.

That's not to say that we don't need to sometimes compromise and play along. But if the bulk of your brand is built on the say-so of others, that's not sustainable. That's not a brand you can live every day, at least not indefinitely.

Tip: Create a brand for yourself that reflects who you are and how you want people to identify you. Then live it every day. It's a lot easier to sell a brand you believe in than one your mama chose for you. Create. Live. Sell.

Faking It

Some people are just nice all the time. They always look for the silver lining. They smile a lot. They're equally kind to friends, colleagues, family, and strangers. It's natural for them.

Some people *act* nice all the time. There's a big difference between being nice and simply acting like you are.

Toya acts nice all the time. She smiles. She compliments. She's effusive. She treats all her acquaintances as if they are her best friends.

They're not.

Toya fakes it. The personality she shows people at work is not at all authentic. Toya has good and bad days like everyone else. She doesn't particularly like every colleague; she finds some offensive.

But she has branded herself as "always happy, always upbeat, always smiling, always agreeable."

Sounds nice, right? The problem is, people don't buy it. They refer to her as "sickly sweet," a term meant to cast suspicion on her motives.

She exhausts people with her over-the-top sunshine.

Here's another downside to her pretending: Toya can never show anyone her true self, her true personality. She reveals very little about herself to her colleagues. She doesn't let them get to know her, so they don't consider her their friend. She doesn't get invited to social gatherings. Conversely, few people accept invitations when she's the one extending them.

Toya is smart and capable. She is optimistic. She does enjoy other people. But either she doesn't have the confidence to show her true colors, or she doesn't trust the people she works with to know anything about her.

Tip: If you are truly as bright as the morning sun every minute of your life, be aware that others might find you disingenuous.

Brand on a Shelf

Have you ever come across something in a store that you absolutely love, but then you got it home and forgot all about it? Don't let that happen to your personal brand.

One New Year's Eve, Hunter spent all day poring over a yellow legal pad, jotting down every characteristic he admires in people who seem to have more active and exciting lives than he does. He decided to adopt as many of those qualities as seemed natural for himself. He curated a brand that positioned him as exceptionally well dressed, funny, outgoing, fun, and friendly with everyone.

He envisioned himself 30 years in the future at his retirement party, when friends and colleagues would recall those very things about him and praise him for his great, social personality.

He told me he wrote his plan down, which, of course, delighted me. Then he told me that he closed his notebook and put it on a shelf in his bedroom. He planned to practice witty things to say, to update his wardrobe, and to book lots of happy hours and game nights with friends and colleagues.

He didn't. In fact, Hunter is pretty funny and can be a lot of fun. But branding himself that way didn't work for him because he didn't sell it. His grand brand plan is stuck on the pages of a notebook he hasn't opened since New Year's Eve. And he's still living a life he considers slow and unexciting.

Your brand is nothing but words on a page or thoughts in your head until you live it. And unless you live it, you can't sell it.

Tip: Tear that page out of your notebook and paste it on your bathroom mirror. Write your brand on your mirror in lipstick. Send it in a text to yourself. Look at it every day. Pay attention to it. Tweak it until it feels livable. Then roll it out.

The Impostor

Perhaps one of the best examples of an imposter—one who got away with it for a long time—is the con artist Anna Sorokin, also known as Anna Delvey, who was convicted of larceny and theft in 2017 for defrauding banks, hotels, and even her friends of $275,000. Sorokin pretended to be a German heiress with a hefty trust fund in order to raise money from financial institutions and wealthy New Yorkers for an art and social club. Along the way, she enjoyed a lavish lifestyle and skipped out on tens of thousands of dollars in bills for designer clothes, fancy hotel rooms, first-class airline seats, and five-star restaurants.

She was arrested after a friend who said she owed her more than $60,000 teamed with police for a sting operation. Sorokin was sentenced to 4 to 12 years in prison, starting with a stay at Rikers Island. She was released in 2021 but taken back into custody a month later on an immigration charge.

Sorokin has sold her story for hundreds of thousands of dollars—and always will be known as a fake heiress who defrauded her friends.

Most people who embellish their brands don't go that far. But if any part of your brand isn't really you, consider why you're trying to sell something that you simply are not.

Blind Spot

In communication theory, the Johari Window model divides personal information into four parts:

1. The information that you know about yourself and that others know about you. This includes information you choose to share as part of your personal brand.
2. The information that others know about you that you might not know about yourself or might think nobody else knows. This is called your "blind spot."
3. The information you keep hidden from others. You might have secrets or bad habits or feelings that you choose to keep private. Sometimes this might lead you to lie or pretend.
4. The information that you don't know about yourself. This could be because of a trauma or simply because you haven't discovered it yet.

When you create a brand, it's important to look at these four windows so you can create a picture of your whole self and of the self you want to present to the world. Pay particular attention to your blind spot: What are you revealing to others without realizing it?

EXERCISE

What does the Johari Window tell you about yourself?

- What is something that everyone knows about you?
- What is your blind spot? What has someone told you about yourself that surprised you?

- What do you hide from others, and why do you hide it?
- What do you still need to learn about yourself? If you don't know, ask for feedback from people you trust.

An easy example is the doctor who insists that patients who smoke wear a nicotine patch until they quit—but he's a closet smoker. His patients can smell cigarette smoke on his lab coat.

He thinks nobody knows, but everybody knows. That's his blind spot.

His brand: "Hypocrite. Not credible. Doesn't walk the talk."

Tip: If you don't realize what people think of you—how people brand you—ask trusted friends or colleagues to tell you the truth. Recognize your blind spots so you can live a brand that counteracts them.

What's in It for Me?

Isaiah spends every Thanksgiving afternoon dishing out turkey and mashed potatoes to long lines of hungry homeless men at a shelter a few blocks from the office where he works. At the end of the shift, he poses with his fellow volunteers for a photo that usually finds its way into his company's newsletter.

He loves the recognition more than he minds giving up his Thanksgiving, finding the pats on the back well worth the sacrifice.

When he spent a Saturday morning with other volunteers painting the activities room of a nearby women's shelter, a reporter and a photographer from a local newspaper showed up. The story that appeared the next day showed photos of a few of the other volunteers, not of him.

He cried. *Cried!*

"Why did I bother wasting a whole morning if my name isn't even in the paper?" he asked himself.

A better question would be, "Why am I selling a brand that is so inauthentic?"

Isaiah isn't a selfless volunteer; he's a shameless self-promoter. How long will it be before someone catches him crying because nobody is helping him perpetuate his ruse?

Tip: If you're selling a brand that positions you as something you are not, ask yourself why. And then make good and sure that you can keep up the pretense, because once you're caught, you're canceled.

Copycat

D.J. walks with a swagger. At parties, he asks for brandy, and on the off chance any of his millennial-age friends keep it in their homes, he won't drink it from anything but a snifter. Who *has* that?

He likes to hold court at parties and meetings, speaking loudly, telling stories about himself and monopolizing conversations.

He's just like his dad, who does the same thing. But his dad has an abundance of natural charm, wit, and confidence that D.J. lacks. So it doesn't translate into "like father, like son." D.J. simply can't pull it off.

D.J. admires his popular father and has fashioned a copycat brand so others will admire him and flock around him when he enters a room. Sometimes they do for a while, but then they grow bored with the egotistical stories that aren't interesting or special.

If you create a personal brand based on the personality of someone else, no amount of good acting will turn you into that person. It's impossible to live a brand that forces you to live as if you're someone else, especially if that act is not in line with your core values.

Tip: It's OK to adopt some qualities of the people you admire—if you actually can adopt them. Pretending can turn your desired brand—"confident, popular, life of the party"—into "poser" or "wannabe."

• • • • • • • • •

To be conscientious about your brand and to make sure you're selling what you intend to sell, you need to get feedback from people you trust to tell you the truth.

Nobody has ever told Margaret that her constant apologizing has made her colleagues respect her less. If someone did, maybe she would stop doing it.

But Margaret has never asked anybody to describe her brand. If she had, she would have been shocked into revising her behavior and selling herself as so much more than her catchphrase.

Do you know which brand you're selling? It's time to find out.

Rebranding

If ever someone needed to ditch an old personal brand and start from scratch with a new one, it was 16-year-old Alfred Yankovic, an introverted college freshman who had spent most of his sheltered childhood alone in his room playing the accordion.

After skipping three grades along the way, Yankovic—you know him as Weird Al Yankovic—wound up as a teenage outcast at California Polytechnic State University—pining to be one of the cool kids on campus but never being able to pull that off.

He tried. Four hours away from his overprotective parents, he rebranded himself as "Al," which, he assumed, sounded cooler than "Alfred." He knew nobody, so nobody knew that he had been two years younger and twice as smart as most everyone in his high school class, had never gone on a date, and spent his evenings listening to radio DJ Dr. Demento, a comedian with an oddball take on music and life.

But the guys in the dorm called him "weird Al" anyway and stole his clothes while he was in the shower. That changed when one of them befriended him and helped him channel his "weird"—and his flawless mastery of the accordion—into a hilarious musical parody show that lit him on fire with popularity.

Today he's a gazillionaire who has sold more than 12 million albums and has fans all over the world.

Yankovic couldn't shake the "weird," so he leaned into it. He branded himself as so weird—a different kind of weird than he grew up with, though—that the college kids, and eventually, millions of fans, consider him the coolest of the cool.

That's what the awkward, geeky introvert from suburban Los Angeles wanted: to be one of the cool kids.

Still an introvert by nature, he rebranded himself as an outrageous geek, and in the process found a way to showcase his enormous talent and his inner entertainer to find success.

Today when people call him "weird," it's a compliment. In fact, that's the name he gave his brand: "Weird Al." "Weird" is what he sells—for lots and lots of money and fame.

IS YOUR BRAND WORKING?

One of the basic principles of personal branding is that everybody has one—even if you didn't choose it, create it, or even know about it.

Seven-year-old Weird Al didn't sit in his room and cook up a brand that would sell him as a weirdo. What kid wants to be considered weird?

He hid in his room and, starting at age seven, learned how to play thousands of songs on the accordion. Perhaps if he thought about branding at all (but, really, what seven-year-old does that?), he thought his brand would be "master accordion player" or "amazing musician." It wasn't, at least back then. It was just plain weird.

"Weird" is what others thought about him, even if that's not how he thought of himself. Others assigned him that brand.

Still, by age 16, he knew he had to rebrand, and he so did. So can you.

IS IT TIME TO REBRAND?

If your brand isn't working for you because it's no longer a good fit—or perhaps it never was—it's time to rebrand.

Here's how to know when it's time to rebrand.

1. Your Brand Has Created Itself

That happens to people who don't believe it's important to consciously and carefully craft a brand that will help them sell themselves. They might not think they have a brand, but they do. Others observe their behavior and listen to what they say and come to conclusions—including many assumptions about the person—right or wrong. In short, others will create a brand for you, whether you like what they choose or not, if you don't create, live, and sell a definitive brand for yourself.

That's what happened to Bradley, a really tall, way-too-skinny college freshman with a high-pitched voice who just seemed to say the wrong thing at the wrong time too often. He interrupted people when it wasn't his turn to talk. He laughed out loud when others around him would think laughing was inappropriate. Sometimes he stood up in the middle of class or during a conversation and walked away, presumably because he was bored.

Although he was smart, very kind, reliable, and interesting, Bradley had few friends. Even the kids he grew up with in his neighborhood didn't know he had these qualities because the immature flaws were so much more obvious.

When Bradley, a brilliant writer, got passed over for the job of captain of the college's debate team, he confided his disappointment in a trusted professor, who gently explained that his personality was holding him back. Others had assigned him the brand of "goofy, inappropriate, and oddball," which is what he was selling, even though he was whip-smart and uber-talented.

With his professor's help, he rebranded. His first move—a pure Bradley move, for sure—was to start wearing thick, black eyeglasses, even though his vision is perfect. He believed others identify those who wear glasses as smart.

Then he ditched his hoodies and high-water jeans (not a fashion statement; he was just too tall for his pants) and started dressing nicer for school. He started counting to three before he spoke, which stopped most of his knee-jerk, sometimes inappropriate reactions to what others were saying. And he quit trying to engage his classmates with his personal stories and instead talked about the books he was reading and the short stories he was writing.

By the time he graduated, Bradley not only was captain of the debate team; he was valedictorian and was selected to make a speech at graduation. He's still a bit of an oddball, but his brand is more "quirky intellectual" than "goofy college kid."

2. You Have Outgrown Your Original Brand

If you were savvy enough to create a brand right out of high school or college that helped you sell your way into a great job, career, or relationship, kudos to you! But the brand that was perfect for you when you were 18 or 21 might not work for the 30- or 45-year-old you.

I was all ears when a young couple who moved into my neighborhood told me the story of how they met.

They went to the same high school, and both agreed that they absolutely could not stand each other. She came from a wealthy family, was sort of spoiled, and made her priorities clothes, boys, and cheerleading, not necessarily in that order. Her brand: "too cool for school."

He rode his bike to school, wore long hair before long hair was cool, and palled around with a group of guys who smoked in the parking lot in between classes, if they even attended. His brand: also "too cool for school," but in a much different way.

They simply didn't run in the same crowd. But when they ran into each other at their 20-year high school reunion—both single parents by that time—it turns out they both had become chefs, and they shared a passion for cooking and traveling.

She traded her spoiled rich-girl brand for one that sells, "I earn what I have." He rebranded from "looking cool is more important than being smart" to "being smart is cool after all."

Chances are good that your life doesn't look the same now as it did when you were starting out. Your brand shouldn't, either.

Regularly updating your brand keeps you in touch with what you want to sell now and gives you the most important tool for selling it.

3. You're Ready for the Next Level

Whether you're ready to go from worker bee to boss, from single to married, from childless to parenthood, or from an established career to a new one, you need to rebrand.

Millions of people came out of the pandemic needing to rebrand after using their downtime during the lockdown to reconsider how happy—or unhappy—they were with their careers and their lifestyles.

Carlotta is one of them. Carlotta was a stay-at-home mom for the six years since her second child was born, after she and her husband had decided she would quit her job as a personal shopper at her favorite boutique so she could raise their kids full-time.

She loved her job, but she loves her kids more. After a stressful semester of pandemic-induced homeschooling and her littlest one's entry into first grade, Carlotta got the itch to go back to work.

This time around, though, she wanted to be a store manager—or at least work her way up to that. She knew clothing stores, like so many other businesses, were having a hard time finding good employees, so she started filling out applications. She expected to get multiple job offers.

She did—but not for managerial positions. The hiring managers wanted her to work as a stylist or a salesperson, and all of them—including the manager at the boutique where she worked six years ago—gave her the same reason: "You don't have management experience."

"Oh, yes I do," she said to herself. Her work running her house and caring for her family had given her the skills she would need to supervise employees, organize inventory, and otherwise see to it that the store operated smoothly.

She needed to rebrand. So she reorganized her résumé into skill sets instead of into a linear timeline of where she worked doing what job. She prepared a list of managerial skills and the specific household and family tasks that require those same skills. She researched the stores' policies, merchandise, and histories so she could offer suggestions for improvement. She bought a beautiful pantsuit from a boutique that was just the kind of shop where she wanted to work—and wore it to every job interview.

It took some doing, but she convinced one store manager to hire her as an assistant manager in charge of inventory and staffing. Her new brand: "manager material."

4. You've Lost or Changed Your Passion or Purpose

I know more than one teacher who left the field of education because of a lack of support from higher-ups and parents. I've met lots of sales reps who burned out after a couple of years on the job because they worked for bosses who pressured them into meeting quotas instead of spending time getting to know clients and their needs.

What seemed like dream jobs when they accepted them felt more like nightmares as the years wore on—and so they changed careers, some pretty late in life.

What they did next: They rebranded.

A career change brought about by disillusionment can be harder than you might think. Teachers, sales reps, and many other professionals attach their identities to their jobs. Unlike Carlotta, who wanted to step up a level in the same field, these people are starting over in new industries, or creating their own businesses, or dropping out of the workforce altogether.

That can call for ditching the old brand and creating a totally new one.

The good news, as you'll read later in this chapter, is that rebranding—no matter how drastically you want to change—draws on the parts of you that never change just as heavily as it incorporates the "new you" that you want to present.

5. You're Stuck

Once you've done the same thing for a long time, others tend to stereotype you into that role. That makes it hard to win a promotion or even make a lateral move, because nobody believes you can do anything besides what they already know you can do.

It happens to actors all the time. Could Olivia Benson (Mariska Hargitay) star in a romantic comedy after playing a police officer on *Law and Order: Special Victims Unit* for 20-plus years? Even in the three TV series that Matthew LeBlanc starred in after *Friends*, did he ever play a character very much unlike Joey? Can you remember seeing Vin Diesel playing anything other than an action hero in the movies—even though he has?

You can get typecast at work as the new guy. You can be remembered for the big project you messed up, even though you've saved the day many times since. You might always be the one who drank too much at one holiday party five years ago or who missed a big presentation by showing up on time at the wrong address. You can even be pigeonholed as so good at one job that there's no way the boss would ever want to move you to another one—even though you want to go.

That's when it's time to rebrand. If you're asking yourself, "Why do they keep telling that story?" especially when you've been trying to change the script, it's time to rebrand.

You can show up to your old situation with a new brand, or you can start fresh with it someplace else. Either way, the only way to get unstuck when others with long memories won't let you soar is to create a brand that will sell you as the person you want to be known as, not the person they knew you as.

6. You Blew It

It happens. Sometimes we go far off brand in a moment of desperation or because of a regrettable lapse in judgment.

Look at America's favorite mom, Lori Loughlin, who played Aunt Becky on *Full House* and the most wholesome characters in a slew of family-oriented Hallmark movies before getting caught paying bribes to get her daughters into a prestigious university.

It's not impossible to recover from an off-brand fiasco, but it's not easy.

Rebranding is usually required in these cases. And the second time around, it's a good idea to choose a brand that you can actually live up to. Remember, branding doesn't stop once you create your brand. You have to live your brand. You have to sell it.

If you do, you might pull it off. I know an event planner who was the administrative assistant in the events department of a large company. She did the detailed logistical work of reserving convention halls and hotel rooms, ordering coffee and food, troubleshooting problems for clients attending the event, and keeping the workflow going for the printing of programs and name badges. Her boss, who was the events manager, spent much of her time marketing the event and nailing down celebrity speakers.

The assistant had started at the company right out of college and had a lot to learn. She learned well, but her colleagues and manager always viewed her as young and inexperienced, even after five years.

When the events manager retired, the administrative assistant was passed over for the job because she didn't have management experience. But she was up to the challenge, so she made herself invaluable to the new manager by dressing, acting, and working as if she, herself, were a manager, too.

Six months later, she resigned from the company and started her own event-planning business. Her first client: her old company. Looks like she sold her new brand pretty well.

7. Opportunity Knocks

Sometimes our lives change in unexpected ways. When that happens, it's time to rebrand.

Nobody has embraced this more gracefully than Olympic gold medalist Brian Boitano.

Brian, who won more gold medals in figure skating than anyone in the history of the sport, leveraged his 1988 Olympic win into a successful career as a professional figure skater. Over the years, Brian has been a sports commentator, written a book about skating, and won a prime-time Emmy award. He has donated much of his time to various charities and started his own charity, a learn-to-skate program for inner-city youth.

At age 46, Brian did a major rebranding, prompted by the animated 1999 *South Park* movie, which featured a song called, "What Would Brian Boitano Do?"

The movie introduced Brian to a younger audience of 18- to 24-year-olds, most of whom had never heard of him.

Brian, always good-natured, embraced the South Park humor and incorporated it into his brand.

He worked with the Food Network to create a show called *What Would Brian Boitano Make?* that featured him cooking for guests in his home. The show ran for two seasons in 2009 and 2010. He used the *South Park* song as the show's theme song. He also wrote a cookbook and has opened a Boitano's Lounge in the Kindler Hotel in Lincoln, Nebraska—one of a series of lounges to come.

As life throws opportunities your way, take advantage of the chance to elevate a part of your brand that you might not have been able to show off while you were busy building and living a brand that made you successful in another area.

And if you're reluctant to make a wholesale change in your life, ask yourself, "What would Brian Boitano do?"

SELLING A NEW BRAND

My tried-and-true, five-step sales process that you'll learn more about in Chapter 10 is just as effective when you've rebranded and want to sell your new brand as it is when you're starting out and selling a brand for the first time.

But when you rebrand, the sale might be more difficult.

The reason? If you have rebranded without relocating, you might have to sell your new brand to the same people who have already bought your original brand, which you did such a good job of selling.

In other words, you're selling against yourself—your old self.

So it is doubly important, when you rebrand, to create a brand that you can live and sell.

To sell your new brand, you have to live it. As you live it, you may face challenges, including the following.

1. You Are Selling Against the Ghost of Your Past

Or at least you're selling against the notion that others have of you, based on the brand you sold them before.

Tip: Expect that this will happen. By living and selling your original brand, you have created expectations for others whom you work or live with. When you rebrand, the ghost of your past brand follows you everywhere you go—at least if you go anyplace where people already know you. Everyone has an image of who you are, and you want to change that image. You want to sell a new image. You want to sell a new brand.

---

2. Any Slip-up Could Reinforce Your Old Brand

Be conscious of the behaviors that others might associate with your old brand.

Tip: Be ready to let go of some of the familiar and even favorite activities that you enjoyed before you rebranded. You don't have to leave everything behind when you rebrand, but you definitely must elevate the part of the brand that will sell you as ready for the next level.

---

3. Living Your New Brand Might Require Some Initial Sacrifices

Say you want to be a stand-up comic. You enjoy doing stand-up routines and often take the mic at small events or at work parties. You've never asked anyone to pay you. But if you intend to make your living as a stand-up, you'll have to start getting paid. As you rebrand, you will only be able to accept invitations for paid gigs.

Tip: Before you can sell your new brand, you have to stop selling your old one.

....

A lot can go wrong when you switch gears as you sell against your old brand, including:

- **Nobody will buy what you're selling.** If you're still behaving as you did when you were selling your original brand, others will not trust that this "new you" is actually the real you.
- **It could be a hard sell.** Convincing others that you can do something they have never seen you do before can be difficult. Use your new brand to prove you have the skill set you need to get where you want to go.

- **Others might not want you to change.** If you're rebranding because you're stuck in a job you've outgrown, you might find that your boss doesn't want you to move. The hard work that got you to the point of rebranding might be making your boss look good, so she doesn't want to move you. Or perhaps she feels threatened by an employee who is grooming herself for a promotion—and she fears you will take her job. Change isn't just hard for the person who is changing. Your new direction certainly will affect others.
- **Others might reinforce your old brand.** No matter how hard you sell your new brand, others might try to sell against you. That is especially true of people who might be jealous of your confidence or success. Someone might spread the word that you're not qualified for what you're going after. Not everyone is happy when a colleague, competitor, or subordinate is on the rise.
- **Without a solid plan, your sale could fail.** In Chapter 3, we explored how to plan and create a brand that you will be able to live and sell. The process is the same when you rebrand: Planning is key. Don't try to sell until you know for sure what you're selling, why you're selling, and to whom you need to sell it.

SOLICIT FEEDBACK

How do you know when it's time to rebrand? Ask people.

Do your friends tell others how great you are? Or do you occasionally hear that someone referred to you in a way that's off brand for you?

Asking for feedback about your brand from others is the best way to know if you're living it as you intend. It's the best way to know if others perceive you the way you hope they do.

When Aki was a kid, her father was an executive of a big company; and every now and then, her father slept late on a workday and left the house at around 9:30 a.m. instead of at 8 a.m. as usual. She asked him if he would get in trouble for being late, and he said he had risen to an important level at the company and he could set his own hours.

Fast-forward 20 years, and Aki is working as a veterinary assistant for a small animal hospital. The veterinarians always compliment her on her techniques and often choose her over the other assistants to help during surgeries.

Aki feels her job is important, so she figured that entitled her to show up a little late every day. Instead of getting there at 7 a.m. like the other assistants, she typically arrived at 7:30 or later.

When it was time for her six-month performance evaluation, the head veterinarian put her on probation and told her if she was late again, she would be fired. He said she wasn't doing her job well because she wasn't there at 7 a.m. to check in the animals arriving for surgery at that time, and that was delaying the schedule for everyone.

Aki's brand, which she thought was "important enough to entitle her to arrive late," actually was "the assistant who can't get to work on time and backs everything up."

She was never late again.

The feedback Aki received shocked her into realizing that her own perception was very different from the perception of those around her when it came to what important people are allowed to do at work. She had no idea others had a negative impression of her.

So she rebranded to "on time, every day."

No matter how consistently you live your brand, it's possible you will rub some people, sometime, the wrong way. It's better to know that than to continue doing whatever you're doing that these people might perceive negatively. It's better to suffer hurt feelings than to continue with a brand that's working against you without your knowledge.

This is why I ask others for feedback. I ask speech organizers to invite audience members to fill out evaluations. I ask clients to tell me how I helped them and how I could have done better. I even ask my friends how I did when I organize a get-together or do them a favor.

I loved hearing about Tomás, the neighbor of my friend Rashida, who volunteers for her neighborhood association. Rashida described Tomás, a young dad who is president of the association, as "truly kind; the nicest person on the block." Tomás asked Rashida to host the neighborhood party in her yard, and Rashida agreed. Rashida, a great planner, blocked the date on her calendar as soon as she made the commitment, which was two months before the party.

Then she planned her month, carefully avoiding conflicts with the party date.

So imagine her surprise when she got an email that Tomás had sent to the whole neighborhood, polling the recipients about which date they would like for the party and where they would like the party to be.

Rashida confronted Tomás, who told her that another neighbor, who had volunteered to play live music at the party, couldn't make it on the original date, so he was searching for an alternative. But Rashida wasn't available any other Saturday that month, having built her schedule around the commitment she had made to host the party. Rashida was upset and told Tomás she felt betrayed.

She and Tomás exchanged a number of text messages. Tomás apologized and restored the original date.

Then Tomás asked Rashida, "Did I respond OK with you?"

Rashida wasn't expecting that. Tomás was asking for feedback so he would know for sure that the issue was resolved; so he would understand if he and Rashida would remain on friendly terms; and so he would know if he handled the situation correctly. Tomás likes to learn from that feedback in case he needs to change his approach—tweak his brand a bit—if a similar situation arises in the future.

What a great brand! And way to live it, Tomás!

Feedback, even when it hurts a little, only makes our brands stronger. Coming right out and asking for it, in fact, strengthens your brand. Someone who is concerned enough about another's feelings and opinions to risk negative feedback is someone whom people want to know and deal with. Tomás's brand, in Rashida's opinion, is "good neighbor."

If you're not soliciting feedback, your brand is not going to grow.

Are you finished growing? Are you finished learning? Are you finished expanding your horizons?

If not, ask for feedback. Ask for it at work, from your friends, and from your neighbors. Then use it to strengthen your brand. If the feedback is critical or persistent, consider using it to rebrand.

If your brand is the sharpest tool in your sales toolkit, then feedback about it is the sharpener that can make it even stronger.

Feedback helps you measure the effectiveness of your brand. It helps you know where you need to soften, strengthen, or otherwise hone the way you present yourself to others.

It will tell you when it's time to tweak, add to, or ditch parts of your brand that aren't working in your favor. It will even let you know when it's time to rebrand.

PART THREE

You Already Know How to Sell

Do you clean your house until it sparkles when people are coming over for dinner or a party? If you use a cleaning service at home, do you take care of especially bad messes yourself before the cleaners arrive?

The last time you got dressed before a first date or a big presentation at work, did you buy a new outfit? Maybe you carefully steamed your best suit and ran out for a quick haircut the day before?

We all do some form of that. We do whatever we need to do to make ourselves look good. We want to put our best foot forward. We want others to think well of us. We want them to admire us for our well-kept homes. We want them to take one look at us and know that we take care of ourselves. We want to show them that we respect them enough to care what they think of us.

We want to sell them on the fact that we look good; we are well prepared; we cherish our possessions and our reputations.

We want to sell them.

In fact, we do sell them. We sell something to someone all day long. We sell our personal brands. We sell our ideas. We sell our skills. We sell ourselves.

You might not call any of this "sales," but that's what it is. Every time you make an attempt to convince another person of anything, you are selling. Whenever you ask for a favor, you're selling someone on doing it for you. If you give the members of your team an assignment, you're selling them on completing it. If you find a lost cat in your backyard and invite it into your warm house for a bowl of cold milk, you're selling.

Here's what a sale is: You want something that someone else can do for you or give to you. You ask, and the other person responds. You are asking that person to buy the fact that you're worth helping. He or she decides. You have made the sale, or you haven't.

Ick, right? You're selling? No way.

That's how I used to feel until I understood that sales does not live up to its suspect reputation. Pretty early in my career, a boss decided I would be a good salesperson and pitched the idea to me. I said, "No." I said, "Never." I said, "Gross."

That boss was a good salesperson, though. He was trying to sell me on changing my career to something he believed I would excel at. I wasn't buying it. But he pointed out the benefits to me and how I could be successful. He asked me to try it, no strings attached.

I did, and I never left. Well, I left that company, but I'm still in sales.

I own a business now. And every day, I sell that business to potential clients. I'm an author now. And every day, I sell people on buying my books by discussing how my topics will help them to get what they want.

I don't manipulate people into signing with my company or buying my books. I don't promise them anything I can't or don't intend to deliver. I don't lie to them. I don't pressure them. I don't do anything cheesy or slimy or manipulative.

Instead, I listen to what they say they need and want, and I respond by telling them what my company or my book can do to help them achieve that.

If they say "no," I say, "Thank you." If they say "yes," I say, "Thank you."

I don't want people to buy anything from me that they don't want or need or value. I want to get what I want by giving them what they want. Win-win.

That's my brand of sales.

The fact is that we sell our way through life and, frankly, through every day. I say all the time that nobody does this life alone. If that's the case, then you need others to help you.

You need to sell others on helping you.

You already do it. In fact, you're really, really good at it. Did you ever go to a job interview and wind up getting the job? Sale!

Have you ever asked someone you like to join you for dinner and then got a yes when you asked for a second date? Sale!

Have you asked a colleague to cover for you while you ran an errand? Sale!

If you didn't get the job, look back at what you sold during that interview. Were you dressed too casually or too formally for the company culture? Were you underprepared to talk about trends and movement in the industry? Did you talk about yourself nonstop during that first date? Did you demand, instead of request, your colleague's help? Were you unwilling to return the favor?

You were still selling, but unfortunately, you may have been either selling something you didn't intend to sell or selling something the other person didn't need or want.

A no in response to your sales pitch isn't a failure. It usually just means you or your product simply wasn't a good fit for the other person.

At least you tried. And you did it with integrity and with concern for the other person. You protected your brand.

It's important that you purposely try to sell your personal brand. You already do it every day, every time you meet or talk or interact with any other person. But that's not always an intentional sale. Make your brand sales intentional.

If you know what you're selling, you live what you're selling, and you're consistent with what you're selling, I guarantee that you will make a lot of sales—and I don't mean of stuff. I mean of you.

Your product—what you're selling—is you.

You already know how to sell. In the next chapter, I'll show you how to sell even better, by using the skills of sales professionals to sell yourself.

First, though, let's take a look at what you've been selling all along without even realizing it.

LIFE SALES

A good friend just told me that her husband agreed—very uncharacteristically—to book a fancy vacation at a high-end hotel in a top-rated resort.

The couple would have to skip their weekly date nights for a couple of months after they returned home and cut back on carryout until they could pay the vacation bill. The husband reminded my friend about that when they were deciding on the vacation, but she kept selling.

She reminded him that they didn't take a vacation the past two summers. She asked him if he noticed how exhausted she was from working all day every day in front of the computer—much of the time on Zoom calls. She convinced him that the two of them work hard, are good at saving their money, and totally deserve to pamper themselves at least once every few years.

They left two weeks later.

Nothing my friend said as she sold her husband on what she considers a necessary expense was untrue. She didn't threaten to give him the silent treatment if he didn't agree to the vacation. She didn't lie or stretch the truth. She didn't cry or try to make him feel guilty.

She simply laid out her case, explaining the benefits of the vacation to both of them and outlining a plan to pay for it.

In the end, he realized how much she needed and wanted this, and he wants her to be happy. She got what she wanted. So did he.

Even if you have never spent a day in a sales job, you sell all the time. You sell when you convince your five-year-old that a bit of crunchy broccoli will taste better if it flies into his mouth like an airplane. You sell when you ask another dad in your kid's carpool to trade days with you at the last minute because you have to get to work extra early on your day to drive this week. You sell when you request a discount at a department store on a shirt that has a tiny stain on the collar. You sell when you ask a friend to spot you a buck so you can buy a snack from the vending machine or when you nominate yourself to serve on your city's Animal Welfare Committee.

I call these "life sales." You're making sales to get what you need and want to get through your day and to live a better life.

Life sales are not professional sales. They're your sales. They're sales you make for you, not for your employer. And if you use the strategies of the sales professional as you attempt these life sales, you'll make far more of them.

Whenever you ask for what you want, you're trying to make a sale. Whenever you get what you want because you asked, you have made the sale.

Sometimes, however, you sell without coming right out and asking for anything.

When a fellow customer at my usual coffee place drove up to the shop one morning in a beautiful Mercedes-Benz, all of us regulars complimented him on it. I could tell he was excited about having it, in part, because it shows off the successful and classy part of his brand.

As a few of us were chatting, I shared that I had been dealing with a plumber that morning over a chronic leak, and I complained about how expensive plumbers are. I quickly caught myself, realizing that the guy with the luxury car probably doesn't worry about how much contractors charge.

But I did make a comment like, "You know how it is, right? What neighborhood do you live in?"

"Oh, I live with my parents," my 25-year-old acquaintance replied. "That's how I can afford to drive this car."

Until he revealed where he lived, he had sold me on believing he was more financially comfortable than I would have expected of someone so young. After he revealed where he lived, however, my impression of him changed.

Still, my point is the same: Like my coffee shop friend, you're selling something that you want others to believe and buy into. You make—or try to make—life sales all day long.

You're not a sales newbie. Get the notion that you don't know how to sell or you're not good at selling right out of your head.

WHAT DID YOU SELL TODAY?

Don't believe that you're a born salesperson who sells all day every day? Try this exercise:

1. Identify life sales you've made in your personal life today. What made them successful?
2. Identify life sales you made at work today. Were they intentional or unintentional?
3. What did you sell about yourself to other people today—both intentionally and unintentionally?
4. How can you sell with more intention at work and in your personal life tomorrow?

EVERY JOB IS A SALES JOB

I understand that just because you're good at making life sales doesn't mean you have any interest in pursuing a career as a professional sales rep.

Do you understand that even though you're not a professional sales rep doesn't mean you don't sell all day every day for the company where you work?

You do sell every day. Even if your job title doesn't include the word "sales" and even if your job description doesn't mention anything about selling, you sell on behalf of your company every day.

And you could sell even more.

Here's what I mean: Say you walk into a doctor's office for an early morning appointment and you give your name to the receptionist, who will let the doctor know you have arrived.

The receptionist greets you with a smile, makes a little joke while she scans your forehead with her electronic thermometer, and invites you to take a seat for a few minutes while the doctor finishes up with another patient.

You sit and scroll through your text messages until a nurse calls your name and walks you back to an exam room.

So far, so good. You might even mention to the doctor how nice and professional the receptionist is. In fact, you might even recommend this medical practice to your friends because you believe the people who work there treat patients with courtesy and respect.

Different scenario. You enter the waiting room and make your way to receptionist's window. She ignores you.

You stand there, waiting. She answers the phone. You clear your throat. She points to a sign-in sheet. You sign the sheet and keep standing there. Without ever speaking to you, she waves her hand to indicate that you should sit and wait. The waiting room is crowded.

So you sit and wait. And wait and wait. Finally, you approach the receptionist again to let her know your appointment time has come and gone. She speaks to you! She says, "You'll have to wait your turn."

You wait a total of 45 minutes. This time, you ask how many patients are ahead of you. She says, "All of them. The doctor isn't here yet."

Stunned and offended, you say you can't wait any longer. She asks, "Do you want to reschedule?"

She's not kidding.

You're gone. And gone forever. You complain to your friends about the experience. None of them will ever go to that doctor's office.

In both cases, the receptionist has sold you something. The first one sold you on a medical practice that delivers a good experience from the minute you walked in the door. You, in turn, sold that practice to your friends by talking about it.

The second one sold you on a medical practice that doesn't honor appointment times and lets patients spend hours waiting for a doctor who may or may not show up. You, in turn, sold against that practice when you told your friends about it.

That receptionist, of course, is not a saleswoman.

Or is she?

That receptionist's job is not to make sales for the medical practice.

Or is it?

She has the power to brand that medical practice as a good one or a bad one. She has the power to sell each patient on coming back again the next time and on recommending the practice to friends.

The word "sales" doesn't appear in her job title or position description. She doesn't earn a commission when a patient returns for a second visit. She doesn't go to sales training or make appointments with clients. She never asks you to buy anything.

But every time she impresses a patient, she makes a sale. In fact, the easiest sales to make are the ones with repeat customers.

And every time she acts rude or dismissive, she loses a sale.

So she sort of is a saleswoman, at least in practice.

In fact, every job is a sales job. It doesn't matter what your job title is. It matters what brand you are selling on behalf of the company every time you interact with a client or potential customer. You can sell people something good about your company, or you can sell them something bad, simply with your behavior.

Receptionist #1 not only sold a positive brand for her medical practice; she sold one for herself. Her brand: "friendly, pleasant, appreciative of your business." Receptionist #2 sold a negative brand for both her company and herself: "rude, dismissive, couldn't care less if you stay, or go, or come back, or call the state licensing board."

Each of them made a sale that morning.

For non-sales pros, these are not necessarily intentional sales. These receptionists weren't trying to sell you on anything—but they both did.

You do that at work, too, whenever you let your own brand shine and bring your best self to a business meeting. Others will associate your competence and demeanor with your company. You sell at work, unintentionally, when you do a good job for a customer, offer service with a smile, go the extra mile, solve a tough problem, or otherwise exceed a client's expectations. Those clients will come back again and again. That makes money for the business.

You also sell when you act cranky, cut corners, or complain about your job within earshot of others. Your customers will associate your bad attitude with the company. They won't come back—and they'll tell their friends, family, and coworkers not to buy from your company. That takes money out of your boss's pocket.

What are you selling at work or about your company, even though you're not officially a salesperson? Pay attention so you don't sell the wrong thing.

As long as you're making unofficial sales for your company—and we all do—why not make some on purpose?

If you're a loan officer for a bank approving mortgages, for example, you have a lot of meetings with Realtors, title agents, and lawyers. At the end of an especially good meeting, why not pass out your cards and ask them all to refer your bank to their other customers?

Customers like to do business with people they know and trust. If their real estate agent or lawyer recommends your bank—or you—to their clients, chances are good that those clients will look you up.

If you sell those colleagues on recommending you, they might sell their clients on doing business with you. That means sales for your company.

A bank manager isn't a salesperson, right?

Wrong.

Everybody is a salesperson. Every job is a sales job. Even if you deliberately shy away from sales, you're still selling.

You're selling a positive or a negative brand on behalf of your company.

SELL YOURSELF

Life sales and unintentional work sales really aren't much different from selling your brand. You can sell yourself and your brand intentionally, or you can leave it to chance and watch your brand sell itself.

As we discussed earlier in the book, a brand that sells itself is a brand that you have not planned, that you do not live, and that you do not bother selling. It's a brand that belongs to someone who believes he or she has no brand, or needs no brand, or assumes the brand is so obvious it requires no effort to maintain.

A brand that sells itself almost always sells the wrong thing.

The fact is that selling the right thing does take some effort. Like the receptionist whose cranky personality sells patients on leaving the medical practice, you can sell others on believing you are something other than what you want them to believe if you don't stay focused on the brand you have planned.

You sell what you don't want when you don't make a good plan for your brand, when you don't consistently live and nurture your brand, or when you ignore your brand and don't even try to sell it.

Create. Live. Sell. One without the others doesn't sell what you intend.

As we've already seen, you know how to sell. You're good at selling. But nothing about selling your brand should be unintentional.

Nothing about selling the most important product you will ever possess—you—should be left to chance.

I hope by this point you understand and believe that you are capable of selling anything—including yourself—if you stay aware of your brand plan and live up to it every day through every interaction you have with others.

In the chapters that follow, you will learn how to sell that brand like a pro.

Don't Sell Yourself Short

Irma's first job out of college landed her at a local TV station as an on-air reporter for a weekend news show. Her friends envy her. Her colleagues want to be her. Her boss adores her.

Like many ambitious young professionals, the first impression she makes—and the second and all impressions after that—is no accident. She knows what she wants from her career and her life. She knows the best way to get that is to portray herself every day as a smart, polished professional. She has created a brand for herself—a way to present herself to the world—that is compatible with her goals to become a successful broadcaster and live an adventurous life as a journalist.

Through her appearance, performance, and behavior, she has lived up to the personal brand she carefully crafted for herself. She sold that brand to everyone she met: "competent, talented, professional—and so very happy and grateful to be part of the weekend news team at the TV station." She worked her magic every weekend for two months. She earned praise and admiration from her bosses and coworkers.

So why, when a weeknight reporter resigned unexpectedly, leaving the job open and available, did her boss pass her over for the promotion?

"I didn't know you wanted it," the boss told her. "I thought you were happy doing weekends."

Irma wasn't unhappy with the weekend shift, but the nightly news is the big time, and that's truly where she wants to be.

It simply never occurred to her that she was selling herself as anything except perfect for the promotion. She never expected that the boss would think she didn't deserve—or want—the more prestigious position.

Her brand was perfect for the job she was in. She followed my model: Create. Live. Sell. But it sold her short when it came to reaching the next level.

As you create, live, and sell a personal brand that will help you get what you want from work and in life, take care that it doesn't stall your progress or limit your opportunities.

Adopt a brand that will get you where you want to go, not keep you where you are. Create, live, and sell a brand that will not sell you short.

SALES PITFALLS

Here are 11 ways you can sell yourself short, even if you think you have the perfect brand.

1. Assuming the Best

One of the biggest mistakes we make when it comes to branding is assuming that others can read our minds.

Like the rising TV news star from the example above, too many of us assume that our bosses, colleagues, spouses, neighbors, friends, and others know exactly what we want even when we don't ask for it.

They don't.

I'm recalling a friend who told me that her husband always asks her for a wish list before her birthday so he can buy her something she likes. But she likes to be surprised, and she feels that after 20 years of marriage her husband should already know what she wants. So she tells him to surprise her.

When he does, she's often disappointed. If he gives her a sweater in a color that doesn't look good on her or a bracelet that's too big, she feels like he hasn't been paying attention.

She rarely gets what she wants because she assumes her husband already knows—or should know. In the process, she sells herself short.

The same goes when it's time to apply for a promotion at work. If you assume you're the obvious candidate so you don't bother applying, chances are good that you won't get the promotion.

That happened to a friend of mine who worked for a small department of a large company. My friend's brand is "laid back, casual, and cool," to the point that people sometimes assume he doesn't care.

In one case, he came right out and said it. He was absolutely the obvious choice for a promotion to assistant manager of his department, which would have come with a steep salary increase.

He didn't apply for the job because he figured it would just be handed to him. Fortunately, another manager encouraged him to formally throw his hat into the ring, so he did.

But during his interview—an interview by committee with a group of managers who all knew him, his work, and his potential—he took cool a bit too far and said, "Hey, you guys know me. You know my work. Hire me if you want. If someone else is better, hire someone else. I don't really care."

And no surprise here: The committee hired someone else.

My friend sold himself short. He was on brand: "cool, casual, laid back." But his assumption that there was no chance the committee wouldn't choose him was far off base. He basically dared his colleagues not to hire him.

Now "shortsighted" is part of his brand.

At least he applied for the job. The husband of another friend forfeited pay raise after pay raise year after year because he never asked for one.

During annual evaluation meetings with the big boss, just about all the employees at his company ask for a raise. They say how much they believe they deserve one and lay out their reasons for saying so.

This guy did not. Instead, he left those meetings empty-handed and insulted that the boss didn't simply offer him more money—lots of it—after observing his hard work and invaluable service for the past year.

It just doesn't work that way.

This employee sold himself—and his family, too—short. His brand is "humble, hardworking, and talented." He believes it goes without saying that he deserves the biggest raise of anyone.

So he never asks for it. His bosses see his brand as "can be taken advantage of," "must not need the money," and "is satisfied with what he already has."

Sure, bosses recognize talent and hard work when they see it. But they don't necessarily recognize a need or desire for a promotion or even a raise if you don't speak up.

Your thoughts do not present themselves as a haircut does: something visible that everyone can see so everyone knows about it. What seems obvious to you—you want to move up, for instance—isn't always obvious to others. When you operate as if it is, you give others too much credit for being able to read your mind, and you don't give yourself enough power and control over your own destiny. You sell yourself short.

In truth, it's a bit narcissistic to assume that others are paying so much attention to you that they know what you want even if you don't ask for it. People are busy, and most of us are too wrapped up in our own work and lives to pay a lot of attention to your world, your reality, and your dreams. Look at it through a different lens: It's just not true that others are or even should be paying close enough attention to you to know what you want.

So if you want something, ask for it. If you're working toward something, tell people about it. For example, let others know which night classes you're taking, which professional and community awards you're winning, and which clients/customers/managers are praising your work.

Make part of your brand, "Here's what I want and deserve." If you don't, you could very well sell yourself short.

2. Selling Satisfaction

Remember Irma, who had her dream job? It was her dream to (1) work at the TV station where she worked and (2) land in the exact position she was working in.

That didn't stop her from dreaming bigger.

Nobody realized that, especially since the evening reporter job became available just a couple of months after she landed dream job No. 1.

She was already living her dream, and everyone knew that. She was living the brand she created for herself. She was selling herself as happy to be where she was.

That brand got her farther than she ever expected she would be just one semester out of college. And that brand got her stuck there.

Her brand was perfect for the job she had. But it sold her short when it came to the next job she wanted.

As soon as you get the job you want, it's time to update your brand so you won't sell yourself short when the opportunity for the next step falls into your lap. As soon as you achieve your dream, re-create your brand so you can sell everyone on believing that you're dreaming bigger now.

Don't live a brand that's perfect for right now. Live a brand that shows you're perfect for what's next.

Here's a look at what can happen if you don't:

Stan's first job after he graduated from high school was as a clerk in the mail room of a fairly large law firm. He sorted and delivered mail to the assistants who handled office duties for the lawyers. He dressed casually for work, the way everyone else in the mail room did, and usually showed up wearing pressed khakis and a clean polo shirt. Everybody liked him. Lawyers even had a friendly nickname for him: "Stamp."

He never minded delivering mail to the lawyers he hoped would someday be his colleagues because he hoped to eventually work alongside them as a lawyer. He had chosen that firm for his first full-time job because as an employee benefit, the company pays its workers' college tuition if their major is in line with a position at the law firm.

So Stan worked in the mail room—eventually becoming its assistant manager—for seven years while he went to college and then law school. And once he passed the bar exam, his dream came true: The firm hired him as an attorney.

Stan dreamed about his first day on the job as a lawyer. He knew he had studied hard and felt prepared to take on his first case. He bought the best suit and tie he could afford on a mail room salary to wear on his first day as a professional.

But something unexpected happened on that first day, and on the day after that, and on the day after that. The lawyers continued to call him "Stamp." They asked him to pick up their mail and their lunch. They were friendly and jovial with him, as they always had been, but they left him out of meetings and never asked for his input.

They treated him as if he still worked in a supporting role as he had for the past seven years.

Stan made one critical mistake before he showed up at work as a lawyer for the first time: He hadn't branded himself as a lawyer. He assumed the other attorneys would automatically treat him like one. They didn't.

A bit of planning could have helped Stan make a new first impression on his old friends. Instead, his old brand—which was perfect for him as he worked his way through law school by working in the mail room—was selling him short as a lawyer.

3. Getting Blindsided

Sometimes your brand can sell you short when you least expect it.

Taylor always loved to cook and has been happy every day since she landed a job as a chef assistant at a local restaurant. She chops vegetables, prepares sauces, takes inventory, and puts together shopping lists so the chef always has the right ingredients. With no formal training, she feels lucky to have a job that she loves.

Her brand is "helpful, happy, engaged, loves to learn, loves to cook."

When the owner sold the restaurant to a chain that doesn't have a chef assistant position, Taylor's brand suddenly made her a mismatch. Still, the new manager was willing to keep Taylor on—if she could do something else.

Because Taylor lacked formal training, the new company wasn't willing to keep her in the kitchen. The new manager offered her a job as a server, which she accepted. But she resigned within a month because it just wasn't what she wanted to do.

Taylor's brand did not include resilience or flexibility, and when she encountered circumstances beyond her control, she couldn't adapt. The new job wasn't offering her opportunities to learn, cook, or be helpful in a way that made her happy.

Taylor's brand sold her short because it was too narrow. She has talents other than food prep, of course, but she never developed them and, frankly, couldn't think of what they were when pressed by the new management.

So she found herself out of work.

The same thing happened to my friend's dad. He worked making a very specialized kind of screw at the same tool and die factory for 25 years and never gave a thought to a future that didn't include that job. He had about seven years to go before he could retire when the firm went out of business during the recession of 2008.

He had no idea what he would do next—so he retired young and struggled financially for the rest of his life. His brand—"very specialized and unwilling to change specialties"—sold him short.

4. Creating a Stereotype

The situation of my friend's dad is not so different from that of actress Meg Ryan, who made a career out of playing the cute and quirky lead in rom-coms but had trouble finding roles once she got older. Or that of the iconic Raquel Welch, who has compared being a Hollywood sex symbol to being a convict. "I was locked in this image and couldn't get out," she said, so other kinds of roles were not available to her.

In both cases, the actresses agreed to play the roles that stereotyped them, and chances are good that they wouldn't have found work if they had declined them.

And whether or not they created those stereotypes intentionally, they became the core of the women's personal and public brands: "girl next door" and "bombshell."

Although both made lots of money and had long, successful careers, those brands sold them short because they may have limited the women's opportunities.

Is there something about your brand that limits your opportunities? Are you stereotyping yourself by keeping the same job for too long even though you would like to do something else? Is there a facet of your personality that others identify you with so strongly that they can't imagine you in any other role?

This kind of unintentional branding can haunt your personal life, too. Does it seem like the men or women you would like to date constantly relegate you to the role of best friend instead of boyfriend/girlfriend? Are you always cast as the wingman/sidekick when you go out on the weekends with your more outgoing best pal? Have you, as an adult, ever been assigned to sit at the kids' table at a wedding or a dinner party? More than once?

If so, your brand is selling you short.

Don't worry; you can fix it.

Rebranding, as we discussed in Chapter 7, is not just for changing careers. It's a way to make a second first impression—or at least to make others forget about your actual first impression. What can you do to replace your reputation as a big kid with a brand that says, "I'm the guy everyone wants to sit with at dinner?"

One answer: Behave like the person you want others to believe you are. Do it consistently. If your brand is casting you in a light that makes you unhappy, change your brand. Then live your new brand. Sell your new brand.

Eventually, it will stick.

5. Treading Water

When is the last time you updated your brand? When is the last time you reconsidered your goals?

Even if you're perfectly happy with your job, your social life, and your home and family, your brand still needs a tune-up every now and then.

If you're still living and selling a brand that you created a decade ago, you could be selling yourself short.

Every couple of years, take an inventory of your brand. Is it still relevant, despite how the world has changed? Do you want the same things as you did before the pandemic? Are your skills up to date, especially in technology?

If the answer to any of these questions is no, tweak your brand.

That might lead you to take a class to sharpen some skills or do some extra reading about trends and methods in your field.

This is important, because even though you might be perfectly satisfied with how things are going for you personally and professionally; you don't ever want to stand still. Part of your brand might be that you're knowledgeable and innovative about your work. So treading water isn't an option if you want others to buy your brand.

Even if you love the work you do and have no intention of changing jobs, it's important to keep your brand up to date. Even if you're standing still at work, for example—that is, you don't want a different job or a different position from the one you've had for five years—you should be putting considerable effort into making sure you don't become a dinosaur.

It takes effort to keep up with the latest trends and changes in your field. If you don't put that effort in—and if you let your brand get out of date—you'll sell a brand of "out of date," "no longer relevant," "old school," or "complacent."

An up-to-date brand helps you compete with those who would like to take your place. Those people might be younger, smarter, better, or more tech-savvy than you are. Do what you can to stay one step ahead so you will remain valuable and irreplaceable.

As you take inventory, ask around—discreetly—to learn how others perceive you. Ask trusted colleagues or clients what they believe your brand is. Use that feedback as your guide to what you need to do to protect the brand you want.

When we don't seek feedback, or take regular inventory of our skills and our reputations, or remain open to change in order to keep up or stay ahead, our brands can sell us short.

Don't sell a brand that gives others the impression you are stuck in your ways and unwilling to change—or haven't bothered to keep up. Ask for feedback, listen to it, and act on it.

6. Playing the Victim

During my years as a college professor, students often asked me to look over the essays they wrote to include with applications for graduate school, internships, grants, and jobs.

Many of them focused on the traumas and tragedies of their lives rather than focusing on how strong they had to be to overcome what had happened to them.

I empathized with these students who struggled to overcome their issues. I admired them for wanting to take the next steps to better themselves.

But I advised them to sell something to these recruiters besides their sad stories.

Their instincts are on the right track: Stories sell. It's good to know your story and to be ready to share it when you're hoping to build rapport and establish trust with someone who might be a position to do you a favor, hire you, offer you a scholarship, or otherwise fill a need for you.

The wrong story, however, can sell you short.

As you craft the story you will use to sell yourself to those people, think about what, exactly, you're trying to sell—and why.

Will having anxiety help you cope with the pressures of graduate school? Will surviving abuse make you a good intern? Does your depression make you more deserving of the grant than the other applicants? Does losing a parent at a young age qualify you for the job?

What is your superpower? If it's that you survived trauma, what did you learn from the experience that will help you cope with graduate school? Did your depression lead you to become an expert in a facet of psychology that you hope to study? Has overcoming poverty to become the first in your family to graduate from college made you a financial expert who wants to help others in your situation find ways to pay for school without taking loans?

Or consider this: Perhaps your past struggles are not what qualify you for the grant or the job. Perhaps your application should showcase the skills you learned from school and work that will help you make your new workplace more efficient or that aided you in creating an innovative way for the company to diversify its staff.

What are you selling? Is your brand "victim"? Is your brand "depressed and anxious"? Is your brand "from a poor family"?

If that is the brand you choose, how about selling yourself as a survivor with a superpower that will help people or companies solve whatever problem you have identified at the company you are applying to?

I recall a former client who grew up in a poor family living in a poor town. She never went to college. Her superpower is that she's scrappy; that is, she can spin gold out of good ideas even when money is tight. Her abilities led her to the sales field, which led her to open a business, which has expanded to five locations.

When people ask her about herself, though, she doesn't say she owns a multimillion-dollar business. She says she grew up poor in a poor town. She sells her poor upbringing instead of her present success—and some people even refer to her as "poor Patricia."

It's important to have a story to tell that will help others get to know and understand you. In sales, it's a given that people like to buy from people they like. Your story can help others identify with you and feel comfortable sharing their own experiences with you. That, in turn, can lead to a sale, such as admission to grad school, a six-figure grant, a new job.

It can also make people feel sorry for you. Is that really what you want to sell?

Do graduate admissions officers select students based on how sorry they feel for them? Do human resources managers hire new employees based on their past troubles?

I don't minimize the trauma and struggles of others. I had to struggle with a few serious setbacks along the way myself. But I don't make that my brand. And my advice to you is to focus your brand not on what you suffered but on what you can contribute.

If that contribution was born of your trauma and you feel comfortable sharing that, by all means, bake it into your brand. If your struggle is what created your superpower, tell your story.

But if that's not the case, consider what you're really selling when you tell it. Consider if it's selling you short because it's taking the place of a different story that could position you as an expert or a perfect fit.

If it is, tell the other story.

7. Going It Alone

Few things in life are as guaranteed as this: Nobody does this life alone.

Even if you're a loner by nature, you're going to need somebody for something some time.

So if your brand is "loner" or even "self-sufficient," you're probably not selling what you think you are. In fact, you could be selling yourself short.

People who insist that they don't need other people generally give the impression that they don't like other people or that others aren't good enough or smart enough for them. People who refuse help when it's clear that they need it often give the impression that they're stubborn, too proud to accept help, or even rude.

That brand doesn't look good on anybody.

I've heard of a young widow who refused to share her feelings with her family or even with her closest friends, saying over and over, "I'm fine." Who is fine after the death of a spouse?

I've heard of a well-educated, 40-year-old lawyer who lost his business because his expertise was in law, not business, and he refused to let family members with business savvy do anything for him.

I've heard of a single mother who can barely feed her children but continually tells neighbors and friends: "I don't need anything." "No, thank you." And even, "Please leave me alone."

Their brands, all of them, are "I'd cut off my nose to spite my face. I'd rather fail than let anyone help me succeed. I don't want to owe anybody anything. We'll starve before we'll admit that we need help."

Yeah, not a good look.

And for what? Pride? A sense that they're selling a brand that says "strong"?

Those brands are selling them short. You can't feed your children with pride, and you can't remain independent for long if you lose your business and won't let anyone help you find another job.

There's absolutely nothing wrong with a brand that showcases your independence or your ability to fend for yourself. Perhaps your core values have led you to that brand. But if that's all you focus on—to the point that you shut others out—you're probably selling a brand that makes people believe you're a snob, or ignorant, or selfish—even if you would never describe yourself that way.

If this is your brand, consider broadening the scope of your brand.

How about this: "Financially independent and able to support myself. Grateful for friends and family. Helpful to others and willing to accept help."

A brand that makes you one or the other is a brand that sells you short. We're all multifaceted people, so our brands, to be successful, also must be multifaceted.

8. Overdoing Humble

Many of us feel that if we talk ourselves up to others, that's bragging. Our parents taught us that. Our teachers taught us that.

They were wrong. Mostly, anyway.

Self-promotion is an important part of my model (Create. Live. Sell.) for a successful and powerful personal brand. If you don't let others know what you're good at, how will they know if you're good at something they need help with? How will they know you're the right person for the job? How will they know you want or deserve the promotion? How will they know to choose you when they need an assistant or a partner? If you don't show others your superpower, why would they choose you over others for the projects, friendships, jobs, and events *you* want?

Please don't say your work speaks for itself. You think it does, but it doesn't. You have to show and tell.

But there's a way to show how awesome you are without bragging. Self-promotion does not have to come off as conceited or egotistic or braggadocious.

The key is to have evidence to support any claim you make about your qualifications, characteristics, or competence.

A friend told me about a colleague of hers, Dr. Stephen Thomas, at the University of Maryland School of Public Health, who is an expert at what he calls "gracious" self-promotion. Nobody would ever call him conceited, because he leads with humility. For the extremely worthwhile events that he organizes, he uses gracious self-promotion as a tool to demystify medical procedures and public health interventions designed to promote good health and prevent disease in underserved, poorly served, and never-served communities.

A public health professor and director of the Maryland Center for Health Equity, Dr. Thomas produces videos and social media posts—starring himself—about his endeavors, such as a program to bring flu shots, vaccinations, and health education to barber shops and beauty salons, which are the hub of social activity in many communities. He recently made a video about his work as a mentor to women and minority scholars in an effort to ensure they knew the difference between "mentors" and "tormentors" and to create a system to match mentors with mentees. And he has used his natural charisma to build the partnerships needed to conduct a free, two-day dental clinic serving thousands—mostly uninsured and in dire need of oral health care.

His bio on the university's website identifies him as "one of the nation's leading scholars in the effort to eliminate racial and ethnic health disparities." That's not bragging; it's a fact.

This is the context in which Dr. Thomas calls what he does "gracious self-promotion."

He lets everyone know what he's involved with, which in turn attracts publicity, money, and clients for the free services he helps to organize. He is prolific on social media. He accepts requests from the media for TV interviews.

He knows he's the best person for that public-facing work. He is articulate and knowledgeable. Most of all, he's passionate about what he's doing.

Sure, his friends, neighbors, students, and colleagues congratulate him on his success. They even rib him about how often they see his face on posters, on TV news segments, and even on flags the university has hung around the city of College Park, Maryland, to showcase its most talented researchers.

But it's not bragging when promoting yourself helps to promote a worthwhile cause. He doesn't talk about how great he is; he talks about how great these services are.

In the process, he has created a brand that speaks volumes about him: "successful, charismatic, leader, change agent, spokesperson for a worthy cause, not afraid to speak up and represent."

I say, good for him.

Maybe we should all engage in a bit of "gracious self-promotion." What's wrong with being transparent and public when you're proud of what you're doing?

Are you proud of your accomplishments? Are you proud of your efforts? Are you proud of your success?

It's OK for "I'm proud of myself" to be a part of your brand. But let's take a page from Dr. Thomas and show our pride graciously and, as often as we can, on behalf of the people our actions benefit. The key is to keep your focus on the honor of serving others.

Don't sell yourself short because you're afraid to show others your superpowers. Don't let your brand sell you short because it's top-heavy with the notion that self-promotion is somehow shameful. Don't sell yourself short by assuming that others will automatically know you've done a good thing just because they've heard about the good thing.

Own your success. Own your superpowers. Like Dr. Thomas, own your brand.

Still can't toot your own horn? Let others do it for you.

One of the best ways to promote yourself is to keep company with people who are happy to brag on your behalf.

My friend, the actor and singer Franc D'Ambrosio, brags about his friends all the time in a way that doesn't seem like bragging at all.

When he introduces me to someone new, he doesn't say, "This is my friend Cindy."

Instead, he says, "This is Dr. Cindy McGovern. She is a *Wall Street Journal* bestselling author."

He wants his friends to know who I am and what I do. He wants the person he is introducing me to to be curious and want to learn more. In his way, he is helping me sell my brands. He helps all his friends in this way.

Franc is known as "The Iron Man of the Mask" because he played the title role in *The Phantom of the Opera* longer than any other performer until recently. He also starred in the movie *Godfather III* and could brag about his slew of awards and accomplishments.

He doesn't. Instead, he brags about his friends. We could all learn a lesson from Franc about how to advocate for our friends.

Part of Franc's brand is "kind and helpful to the people around me." I'm so grateful that Franc is willing to introduce me the way he does, because although I'm good at living my brand, bragging doesn't come easy for me.

By living my brand, I give others stories that they can share about me.

I'm OK with that. I'm honored when my friends or colleagues are willing to talk about me.

In return, I love to help others to promote their brands. Maybe this is karma?

9. Not Choosing a Brand

Nothing sells you shorter or faster or with more negative consequences than the brand you did not plan for. Nothing sells itself more easily than the brand you think you don't have.

You are deluding yourself if you believe:

- You do not need a personal brand. (You may have picked up this book because someone suggested that you actually do need one.)
- You do not have a personal brand because you never created one.
- You do not need to create a personal brand because you simply are who you are.
- There is really no such thing as a personal brand.

If you suffer under any of the above beliefs, give me a few paragraphs to convince you of two things:

1. You do have a personal brand, and everyone knows what it is but you.
2. You need to create a personal brand so you can be the one deciding what it is rather than leaving that decision to the assumptions of others.

Let me tell you a story about Raj, who is charming, intelligent, carefree, and interesting. He's still in school, studying for an MBA at night while he works full-time as an office assistant at a company that promotes environmentally friendly products. Raj wants to be a marketing professional at this company more than anything else. He has been encouraged by a couple of account reps who complimented his ideas and enthusiasm when he assisted them with cases.

But he thinks his job as an assistant is beneath him. He doesn't like typing, filing, taking notes, looking stuff up for others, scheduling appointments, or ordering office supplies. He wants to work with clients and the media.

So he doesn't rush to work in the morning and often straggles in a little late. He wears jeans and sneakers to work sometimes. He complains when he's assigned to do office work. He spends a lot of time on social media while he's sitting at his desk.

When he overheard one of the account reps singing his praises, he was dismayed by the comment that finished the conversation: "Too bad he's so unprofessional. We can't have someone like that working with our clients."

I asked Raj to describe his personal brand. He replied, "I don't have one."

Oh, Raj! Yes, you do.

Yes, Raj has a personal brand: "unprofessional." And everyone knows it but him.

He thinks his brand is "smart, creative, marketing pro of the future." But instead of living that brand and selling that brand, he's selling "stuck up, lazy, and unprofessional."

He's not trying to sell that negative brand. He's not trying to sell anything. And that's the problem.

If you do not create, live, and sell your personal brand, others will assume one for you and associate it with you, assigning one to you on your behalf. And you're probably not going to like it.

Others will observe your unprofessional behavior and, in the absence of any effort from you to sell them that you are, indeed, professional, they will brand you as unprofessional.

It's as simple as that.

Most of us think the best of ourselves. We think we present ourselves in a positive light. We believe people think we're smart, fun, funny, a pleasure to be around. We assume people can see our talent, recognize our gifts, appreciate our competence.

We couldn't be more wrong. Assumptions almost always are wrong.

The fact is that we don't really know what others think about us unless they tell us—and even then, not everyone is completely honest about it. People might say we're great because they don't want to hurt our feelings, or because they believe if they flatter us, we can do something for them in return.

How do you let people know about your brand? They know already.

Recognize the fact that you've got a brand whether you chose it or not. You have to let people know you've changed your brand. You've got to sell it.

10. Underselling Your Superpowers

One of my close friends has an amazing superpower that allows him to explain the most technical information in plain, easy-to-understand language. He is a tech wizard who has worked as a product manager for various companies over the years. Not only does he know his products inside and out—literally, he knows what every wire and inner component does—but he can describe what all of that has to do with a problem a customer is having without using jargon or talking down to anyone.

This friend is in the market for a job change. On paper, his brilliance shines like the sun, so he has been invited to interview for six jobs so far. He didn't get any of them.

Here's what's going on: My friend is not showcasing his superpower during the interviews. Instead, he is politely answering each question the interviewers ask without adding any information that wasn't asked for. As a result, the interviewers aren't getting a proper sense of how special this guy is and how much he could benefit their companies.

My friend is selling himself short by keeping his success stories to himself. The interviewers don't know he has the magic touch with less-than-technical customers—and sometimes with confused coworkers who benefit from his easy explanations. The interviewers don't know this because he hasn't told them.

Don't keep your superpowers to yourself. Share them with potential employers, coworkers, customers, and even friends and acquaintances who might recognize what an asset you would be if you came to work for them.

11. Not Owning Your Block

Once you choose a brand, own it.

There's a saying in sales: "You own your block." Basically, that means nobody should be selling in your neighborhood. Nobody should be selling your product better than you. Nobody should know your product better than you.

It's the same when you sell your personal brand. Create it and then own it. Own your identity. Own who you are and what you're selling. Own what you bring to the table. Own your superpower.

Then live that brand and sell that brand like nobody else can. If you know someone with a similar brand, outsell that person. Own your block.

You sell yourself short when you undersell yourself.

I met a young woman at a sales conference who had just bought the business she worked for and was there for a sales workshop. The first question I asked her: "Why doesn't your email signature say 'owner' under your name and your company's name?"

The woman said she didn't want to come off as pretentious, as she had only recently become the owner and had never owned a business before.

I told her to brag. She was underselling herself as a business owner when, in fact, she was able to buy a business at a very young age. That's a selling point. Use it to sell.

Own your block. Own your success. Own your title. Own your brand.

10

Sell Like a Pro

The most successful sales professionals I know follow a fairly simple sales process to sell everything from clothes to insurance to houses to personal services. And why wouldn't you want to adopt the most effective strategies of sales professionals to make the most important sale of your life?

Below is the simple, straightforward sales process I use—five easy steps to sell yourself and your brand:

STEP 1. Plan for the sale. Of course. I'm all about planning, and for success in life, you should be, too. Once you have your brand plan in place, use it to plan for its sale.

STEP 2. Look for opportunities to sell your brand. Once you start looking, you'll see them everywhere. You'll find people who can help you advertise your brand. You'll become aware of events that will help you showcase it. You'll be able to put yourself into situations that allow you to network with people who are looking for an employee, partner, consultant, or personality just like you.

STEP 3. Establish trust with the people you want to buy your brand. Get to know them, and let them know you. Listen to what they need to determine if your brand is a good fit for an open job they might have or for a spot on their committee. Show them who you are by consistently living your brand so they know they can count on you.

STEP 4. Ask for what you want. Do you need help getting the word out about your new brand? Ask others to talk about you and your new brand. Does someone you know work at the company where you want to work? Ask for an introduction and a recommendation. A strong, consistent brand will bolster your confidence to go after what you want and deserve.

STEP 5. Follow up with consistency and gratitude. A brand that's just for show might get your foot in the door. But once you're inside, you need to live the brand you sold to those who helped you get in. Show your gratitude by following through on everything you promised. Show your gratitude by being the person your brand promised you would be.

The following sections will unpack each of these five steps with examples and helpful tips. But before we begin, it is important to reiterate why a sales plan is vital.

WHY A SALES PLAN?

Your personal brand will not sell itself, with one exception. If you don't create and live your personal brand, you will leave the decision about who you are and what you can be up to others. In other words, your lack of a brand means you're not in control of the sale.

Creating your brand isn't enough. You need to live it. You need to sell it.

Create. Live. Sell.

Selling your personal brand is the most important of these three crucial steps. If you create a brand and don't sell it, you've wasted your time.

Like most things in life, the sale of your personal brand is far more likely to go well if you plan for it. In fact, the sale is far more likely to happen at all if you plan for it.

Too often, we have a great idea that we forget about or push to the side because we haven't spent the time or thought required to get it off the ground. We decide to make every Friday a date night but we don't put it on the calendar, so Friday comes and goes. We talk about taking that dream vacation, but we don't put anybody in charge of research, reservations, and scheduling. We never go.

Don't let your personal brand sit on your shelf. Live it every day. Sell it to everyone you interact with. Put it to work for you and your goals.

Sell it.

Your Best Sales Tool

Living your brand consistently and with intention is the best way to sell your brand, which, of course, sells you.

It might help for you to type up a list of your brand's greatest hits and tape them to your computer, refrigerator, or bathroom mirror, or put them in your phone. That way, you will constantly remind yourself of your greatest goal: to present yourself to the world in a way that you believe will get you what you want and where you need to be.

At my brand's core are the qualities I want others to identify me with: professionalism, kindness, generosity, honesty, helpfulness. When those words stare me in the face every morning as I dress for the day, I start to think about them even before I leave for work. I'm reminded that it's important for me to be nice to others and to make sure that the consulting services I hope to sell should be helpful to my clients and not just profitable for me. It reminds me of how I want to present myself to the world.

Of course, those values are deeply ingrained in me, so they come naturally. Still, it helps to be reminded of them at the start of my day, which could throw an angry client or a frustrating situation in my path and tempt me to react in an off-brand way. When my core brand values are top of mind, they're easier to stick with no matter what.

THE FIVE STEPS

Here is an in-depth, step-by-step look at my five steps to sales success.

STEP 1. PLAN FOR THE SALE

To effectively sell yourself and your brand, you need two solid plans.

The first is a thoughtful plan for creating your brand, which you learned about in Part One of this book. The second is a detailed plan for selling that brand.

The brand plan comes first. Then the sales plan. They're different plans; yet your sales plan relies heavily on your brand plan.

As you created your brand, you looked inward to discover who you truly are, which of the many facets of your personality you want others to identify you with, and how you might reasonably, sustainably, and authentically present yourself to the world.

To create your sales plan, you will look outward. You will determine:

- Which actions you need to take to convince others to buy the brand you are selling; that is, how you will persuade others that what they see is what they get.
- Who can help you do that.
- Where to find opportunities, like networking events and introductions to influential people, that will introduce you and your brand to those who can help you reach your goals.

- How you will use your personal brand to differentiate yourself and make yourself memorable.
- When to elevate different facets of your brand. For example, selling your brand at work might be different, at least in some ways, from selling your brand socially or at home.
- How to use the skills of the professional salesperson to sell the most important product you have: yourself.

How to Plan

Chapter 3 discusses how to plan your brand. This chapter is about creating a plan for selling your brand. They're not much different.

Here are some best practices for creating a sales plan:

- **Schedule time to think.** Unlike your brand plan, which relied on your thoughts, feelings, perceptions, and personal goals, your sales plan will require you to do research, schedule actions, and create checklists.
- **Write it down.** Any plan is more effective when you write it down and look at it often. Without the words on a page, a plan is really just an idea. Make your plan solid.
- **Outline your goals.** What do you want to accomplish with your personal brand? Do you hope to repair your reputation or create one that shows you in a new light? Will you use it to land your dream job? Could your brand help you find your way into a new social group? Are you using it to position yourself as the expert in your field or at your company on a certain topic?
- **Make lists.** Who can help you? Which professional or social groups should you join? Where are the job openings

for the position you want? How can you use your personal brand to sell your way into those jobs?

- **Create subplans.** Different situations and goals sometimes call for you to elevate different parts of your brand. As you plan for each new encounter, plan for how you will showcase different parts of your personality, expertise, or experience as part of your brand sale.
- **Focus on your strengths.** Plan how you will use your brand to differentiate yourself from others whose goals are the same. This is where sales come in. Sell yourself as different, more, and better. If you're not standing out, you're not going to be memorable. A good exercise: Dust off your high school yearbook. Which people made a lasting impression on you, and which ones do you remember absolutely nothing about? Why is that?
- **Schedule action.** Even a terrific plan won't help you sell your brand if you don't execute it. For every name on your list of people who can help you, look up an email address—and then send an email. For every networking opportunity, write it on your calendar—and then attend. Make checklists of the activities you need to do to put each part of your plan into action.
- **Keep your plan handy.** Don't write your plan and hide it in a drawer. Keep it someplace where you will refer to it often.
- **Track your progress.** Check off each goal as you accomplish it, and add new ones as they come up. More importantly, use your plan to monitor your progress. Are you selling your brand? Are those sales moving you closer to your goals?

- **Monitor your brand behavior.** Use your plan to check yourself if you get off track. Keep tabs on how often—and why—you go off brand. If part of your brand is "nice" and you treated someone with impatience or cynicism, why? If you have branded yourself as professional and you've been dragging into work later and later each day, what's going on? Use your plan to evaluate any off-brand behavior and inspire you to live and sell your brand more consistently.
- **Update your plan.** Life can throw us curveballs and also offer unexpected opportunities. Don't let your plan hold you back. Add facets to your brand. Change your focus. Accommodate new dreams. A brand is a living, breathing thing, and your plan should be, too.
- **Plan before you act.** Like a brand plan, a sales plan starts with knowing exactly what you are selling. It's critical to create your sales plan first—before you start to sell your brand. Avoid the temptation to offer a "sneak peek" when it comes to selling your brand. You need a solid brand plan and a solid sales plan, both of which will help you sell exactly what you intend to sell. There are no presales when it comes to unveiling and selling your personal brand.

STEP 2. LOOK FOR OPPORTUNITIES

Your personal brand shouldn't exist only in your head. In order to become known for something, you need to show it to others. You need to live your brand. You need to sell your brand.

Once your brand plan is solid, it's time to take your personal brand out for a spin. Start by looking for opportunities to unveil the new you and sell the brand you want others to buy.

How to Find Opportunities

As soon as you start looking for opportunities to sell your brand, you will find them everywhere. As you begin to use your brand to sell yourself, you might find the following list helpful.

1. Live Your Brand

Conducting yourself according to your brand some of the time rather than all of the time will not solidify your brand. In fact, it will create a new one for you—as someone who is faking it.

Sure, most of us do a little bit of faking it when we start something new. We might be nervous, but we pretend to be confident. We might be unsure that we can pull off a new brand, but we put on our game face and try.

That's different from being inauthentic. It's being a good salesperson. You know you're good at this, but you also know you're new at it. Act like you've been doing it all your life. Pretty soon, that won't be an act.

Still, if you want your brand to stick, your behavior must jibe with it

One of the most inspiring women I've met is Shelley Zalis, the founder of The Female Quotient, an organization dedicated to gender equality.

I believe there's nothing anyone could say to Shelley to make her deviate from her message of "the time for equality is now."

Shelley isn't a saleswoman, officially, but she spends her time selling the world on the need for women and men to be treated equally in the workplace and in life.

My favorite story about Shelley: She put together a panel of women leaders to speak at a conference for other women.

When I spoke to her afterward, she offered to help me in any way she could. People sometimes say that without meaning it. Not her. She's been helpful so many times since. And along the way, her voice has been powerful and consistent as she helps women find success.

2. Put Yourself Out There

If you have a personal brand, let people know. Look for opportunities to showcase your newly branded self.

Examples:

- If you want to be a social media star, then be present on social media. Tweet, post photos, offer advice, and comment on news relevant to your field—or whatever your brand is related to. Post videos of yourself making speeches, being interviewed, or offering your perspective on relevant topics. Accountants, lawyers, contractors—people who work in all sorts of industries—are going online to promote themselves as influencers in their fields. This is equally true for Uber drivers, aerobics instructors, freelance graphic designers, and others in the gig economy who are trying to create a following of loyal clients by promoting themselves online and collecting as many positive customer reviews as possible. This is the equivalent of the "brand portfolio" that professional salespeople compile to showcase the products and services that they sell. Your product is you. Your product is your brand. Gather evidence to back up what you're selling.
- If your brand has more to do with shining in the office than starring online, behave as you would if you already have the job you aspire to. Grab the opportunity to make

speeches and write articles. Say yes whenever you're asked to share your expertise by sitting on a panel, joining a board, giving a media interview, conducting a workshop, or training the newest member of your team. Branding is a pursuit best carried out in public. The more you can showcase your knowledge and confidence, the more people will seek you out as an expert in your field.

- See and be seen. If you're not attending conferences, not accepting invitations to professional and social events, and otherwise not showing up where the people who can help you succeed can see you and get to know you, you're not selling. Get out there and talk about your field, demonstrate your expertise, meet influential people, and become a fixture at the events where others with similar goals network. Selling your brand isn't a game of hide-and-seek. If you hide from public view, nobody will seek you out. Instead, position yourself as someone who is expected to be there so you will be sorely missed on the rare occasions when you are absent.

3. Share Your Brand Plan with People You Already Know

These people can become your first—and most loyal—followers or advocates. If you're a mom who is starting a child-rearing blog or household hints show on YouTube, for example, brand yourself as an expert by introducing your advice to the moms in your neighborhood. Not only will they spread the news about your new brand/blog/videos to their friends and family; they can offer you valuable feedback on your initial pieces and shows that might help you make them even more useful. If you're a mid-level manager with the hope of a promotion, brand yourself as a rising star with your coworkers by taking a leadership role on team projects and being a resource for colleagues with questions.

4. Identify the "Big Mouths" in Your Company or Field

If you have the attention of these formal and informal leaders in your workplace, they can help you promote and solidify your brand. If they become your advocates, they will spread the word about you. Network with them. Find a way to work with them. Impress them. And stay on their good side. The big mouths can ruin your brand as easily as they can help you build it.

5. Find a Mentor

Attaching yourself to a more experienced, branded colleague will help you accomplish two things. First, you will learn a lot about how to succeed from a willing mentor/coach/advocate. Second, you will attach your reputation to your mentor's, which could give you more credibility.

Nobody does this life alone, and that includes branding. Hitch your wagon to an older, more experienced star in your universe, and follow the lead of someone who has "made it" the way you want to.

6. Change Your Business Card (Literally or Figuratively)

You might temporarily be a business assistant, a college student, or a cashier, but that's not your brand. Your business card, along with your social media and any publicity you might get, should identify you as the person you want others to see.

An accountant who has a huge social media following because of his tax advice video might title himself as an accountant and social media influencer or even a celebrity accountant. A rising accountant with no social media aspirations might identify himself as a financial expert or an accounting advisor.

While I was planning my first book, *Every Job Is a Sales Job*—but before it was published—I tweaked my brand, my LinkedIn page, my website, and my business cards to add the brand word "author." Find a branding word to add to the things that identify you so it's clear to everyone that you're moving up.

7. Defend Your Brand

Just as you'll want to jump on every opportunity to let people—those in your circle and in the public—know you are an expert/influencer/advocate or whatever your brand is, grab every chance to defend your brand when someone questions it.

Once you reveal your brand, things could start changing in your world—for the better. That could make others jealous or competitive, especially if they have been working on their brands longer. When someone lies about you, disrespects you, or calls your qualifications into question, respond—with logic, an even temper, and facts about your own value. Never argue, get defensive, or go on the attack; that would go against your brand. Instead, stick to the facts, be nice, and assure everyone that you have what it takes.

But don't let it slide. Don't let anyone cast doubt on your brand without stepping up to set the record straight. Fiercely protect and defend your brand.

Everyone knows someone like Janie. She works in a testing lab at a hospital in the small city where she grew up. She's brilliant, but she keeps her head down, works hard, and doesn't rock the boat at work. She's shy but well liked, and she's comfortable in her professional and social life.

One day, everything changed.

While doing some routine lab tests, she noticed an unusual mutation in the antibodies from multiple patients who all suffered from the same symptoms. She pointed it out to her supervisor, who ran it up the chain of command to the lab manager.

Long story short, two years later, the lab manager and a physician who specializes in mutations collaborated on a paper for a medical journal and took credit for Janie's discovery. It was scheduled to be published by the end of the year.

Friends comforted Janie and told her she deserved to be recognized for her work. They said they were sorry. They badmouthed the lab manager.

One friend took a different approach. This very good friend told Janie this was bound to happen. She described her dear friend as "a doormat" for letting people walk all over her—for allowing her efforts to go unnoticed and uncredited. She said people take advantage of Janie because she's selling them on the fact that it's OK to do that.

Janie believes her brand is "cooperative, kind, helpful, team player, the wind beneath everyone's wings."

Her good friend knows Janie's brand is "I don't need or want to be noticed." And many people read that as an invitation to take what she won't—all the credit.

She helped Janie realize she needed a new brand, one that sells, "I stand up for myself."

Janie is still collaborative, a team player, kind, and helpful. Those wonderful qualities are at the core of her brand. But now, she decided, she'll be one more thing: "assertive."

She sold that new brand by doing something totally off brand for the old Janie. She went to the publisher of the journal and reported her colleagues for stealing her work.

STEP 3. ESTABLISH TRUST WITH THE PEOPLE YOU WANT TO BUY YOUR BRAND

The true intersection of branding and sales lies in trust. If people like you and trust you, they will buy your brand and help you on your way to success.

No matter how well you brand yourself, selling that brand hinges on the level of trust you inspire for yourself in other people. So make trust an integral part of your brand. Make it the facet of your brand that you sell the hardest.

Don't wind up like Guy, who seems to have no clue that he routinely offends the people he works with and speaks to.

Guy is a sales manager. His motto is "Buy from Guy."

He's tone-deaf. He's clueless. He's . . . something else. There's no word to express the depth of how "off" his brand is.

For starters, Guy thinks he is hilarious. He thinks people really like him. He's outgoing and always smiles. He smiles even when he's looking right at you and demeaning you. Usually that "you" is a woman.

Guy has no idea how to read a room. He recently traveled with a female colleague—a friend of mine—so the two of them could deliver a presentation to a roomful of sales representatives. The audience was almost evenly split between men and women.

He spent the first 20 minutes of his presentation making jokes at the expense of people in his audience. He belittled the women in the room, saying they "can't sell their way out of a paper bag." He called female clients "pushovers" and "professional pastry peddlers."

He was joking, but his jokes fell flat. Nobody laughed. In fact, some people stood up and walked out of the room.

When my friend told me about this, her face turned beet red. She didn't want to say anything to him publicly, but she knew the audience wasn't going to enjoy her part of the presentation, either, because she had come to the convention with Guy.

That nobody in the audience laughed and people started leaving early should have told Guy that he was doing something wrong. But he thinks an audience that doesn't laugh at his jokes simply has no sense of humor.

He believes his brand is "funny, great salesman, friendly, guy's guy."

The audience and my friend believe his brand is "offensive, unaware, chauvinistic, insensitive." They don't trust him. And according to my friend, he made zero sales during that trip.

It's hard to trust a guy like Guy. Building trust starts with understanding what others need from you. Guy doesn't bother to find that out—possibly because he subscribes to the oldest of outdated sales tactics: Sell what you want the customer to buy.

In this case, Guy was trying to sell himself, and the customer was the audience he came to talk to.

He sold himself, all right, but not in the way he intended. And he doesn't even know it. And to tell you the truth, he probably doesn't care.

Read the Room

Whether you're selling your brand to a single person, like a job interviewer, or to a group, say, of colleagues you are presenting to at work, you can succeed where Guy failed by figuring out what the people you're selling to actually need from you.

In what way can you help them? In what way could the personal brand you're selling benefit them?

My favorite sales method is a consultative approach to sales. Instead of pushing what their companies want them to sell, professionals who use this method get to know their customers a little and try to figure out what they want or need to buy.

They listen. They ask questions. They learn about the customer's problems and needs. Then they determine which of their companies' products might solve those problems or fill their needs.

In short, they create a win-win for themselves and their customers. They sell something, which is a win for the sales rep and company. The customer buys a product or service that is needed and wanted from a sales rep whose brand is "helpful and responsive" rather than "pushy" and "me, me, me." Both walk away happy.

Listening, observing, and focusing on the other person or people you're with is all a part of reading the room.

Reading the room is way to pay attention to how people react to you. And responding to that reading often means you need to adjust your script when that reaction is unexpected.

A personal example: I recently led a series of sales workshops in the South. I met a few folks at one of my workshops who seemed to believe that consultants from California—I live in San Francisco—don't understand what is important in making sales and cultivating relationships in the South. To try to connect with the people I met there, I explained that I am originally from the South and have lived in Florida, Georgia, and Tennessee.

The mood in the room changed. I was no longer the lady from the big West Coast city who did not understand how business is conducted in their part of the country. By reading the room, I was able to connect with the audience members, who then seemed to be more willing to embrace me as friendly and as "one of them" because I shared a little bit about my past with them.

I elevated my experience into my personal brand at the moment I needed it. I suspect, though, that they would have figured it out as soon as "y'all" fell out of my mouth for the first time.

I gave them what they needed: a reason to trust me. And I got what I needed: their trust.

Win-win.

Whether you're a teacher, a retail clerk, a politician, a social media influencer, or an entrepreneur offering services one-on-one to potential clients, pay attention to what the other person is saying and asking for. Pay attention to how people react to you—to what you're saying and how you're behaving.

And don't just read the room; react to it. If the vibe is negative, change course. Your personality is multifaceted. If you have created a solid personal brand, then your brand is multifaceted. Elevate a different facet—one that might resonate or feel more agreeable to the person or people you're speaking with.

Be Consistent

Think about the people you trust the most: your partner, a certain coworker, the neighbor who babysits your children, your parents.

Now consider why you trust them.

Maybe it's just a gut feeling, and that's certainly something to pay attention to. But chances are good that your trust has grown over time as these people have consistently proved to you that they are reliable, responsible, honest, and accountable. They have your best interests at heart. They never let you down, at least not on purpose. You can count on them.

Now think about the people whose trust you want. Some of them are strangers or colleagues who know little about you except that you're good at your job.

Why should they trust you?

The answer to that question is the same as the reasons why you can trust others. Your colleagues, boss, neighbors, and even the strangers you address in your audience will trust you if you have consistently demonstrated that you are trustworthy.

At work, do you show up every day, ready to pitch in? Do you meet your deadlines? Do you give 100 percent? Do you respect your colleagues? Are you even-tempered? Do you own your mistakes?

Can people count on you?

Do you sell a personal brand that convinces them they can count on you? Trust you? Believe you?

If you live your brand consistently, people who work with you, live near you, attend your presentations, or otherwise interact with you will know if they can trust you.

If your brand is "wild," "sporadic," "risk taker," or "unreliable," you're selling others on the fact that they can't count on you. But if it's "consistent, reliable, respectful, and accountable," you're selling trust—and they're buying it.

Would the people you're hoping will trust you leave their children in your care? Would they stake their reputations—or their company's good name—on your work and on your word?

What if the roles were reversed?

A key to trust is consistency. Make "responsible" and "trustworthy" part of your brand—and live it. If you do, trust is easy to sell.

Protect Your Reputation

Nothing solidifies you as a trustworthy friend, employee, coworker, influencer, speaker, thought leader, rising professional, or advisor quicker or more solidly than a good reputation. And nothing can break your brand faster than a bad one.

Here are 10 important ways to protect your reputation, which, in turn, will protect your brand.

1. Control the Narrative

Keep control of your own story. Don't put anything in the public domain that you are embarrassed about, are ashamed of, or are not sure of or that isn't well thought out. Tell only what you want to be retold, tweeted, posted, or reminded of far into the future.

2. Guard Your Private Life

I post very little personal information about myself on my websites or social media. In fact, I rarely tell my personal business, even to employees, clients, colleagues, or vendors. They know that I'm married and that I have a dog. But I don't talk about my husband, my problems, or feelings that I share only with friends. Part of my brand is "professional and businesslike." It's not businesslike to talk about my marriage, my finances, my family, or my social life. My private life stays private.

3. Keep Your Social Media Clear of Political, Racist, Sexist, and Phobic Comments, Photos, and the Like

Something your immediate circle of close friends finds funny could be offensive to a more general audience. Even if you have privacy settings on your nonpublic accounts, there's no guarantee that someone won't share the post.

4. Don't "Use" People

When coworkers agree to cover shifts for you, do you return the favor when they ask you to do the same for them? If a colleague agrees to talk you up to the boss when you're hoping for a prime assignment, do you also put in a good word for him when he's in line for something special? Building a brand as a team player, a good friend, and someone who's willing to speak up for what's right can go a long way toward moving you to the next level in your career. I say it all the time: Nobody does this alone. Do for others if you would like them to do for you.

5. Be Authentic

It's perfectly clear to everyone when you are networking just to network. If you're not genuine about getting to know people and about using your brand to help others and not just yourself, your brand could backfire. And avoid aligning yourself with users. People like that won't be loyal followers, or recommend others to your social media sites, or be your true supporters. And your advice won't feel credible or trustworthy to followers who do treasure relationships.

6. Show, Don't Tell

You can tell people all day long that what you have to offer is valuable, or that you are trustworthy, or that you deserve their loyalty. That won't convince them, though. You have to show them. You can do that by consistently taking the needs of others into consideration; by using your brand and your influence to help others; by doing what you say you will do; and by keeping your promises. Someone who tells others, "You can count on me," will build a brand of "reliable" only if she comes through every time.

7. Be Transparent and Honest

Some influencers attract social media sponsors, who pay them to mention their products or send them free clothes or recipe ingredients to talk about on their shows. The best of these influencers reveal the sources to their audience when the influencers are about to gush over—or criticize—a product they have received for free. The ones who are not transparent about that will risk their reputations if viewers or competitors find out and assume that they are promoting things just because they got them for free. Their brand: "sellout."

8. Keep Polite Company

Your choice of friends can say a lot about you, especially at work. If your brand is "mature, responsible, and ready for promotion," but you hang out with a group of coworkers who don't seem to take their jobs seriously, who do the minimum required, who show up for work looking like they haven't slept or showered, and who spend too much time socializing or texting during work hours, the bosses will think you're that way, too. It's a sort of ripple effect.

It's OK to be friends with colleagues, but don't let work become all about your friends. Instead, reserve your chats, parties, and inside jokes for after hours. Likewise, avoid associating with coworkers who seem to dislike their jobs or the company you both work for. Employees with a reputation for complaining and bad-mouthing the work or the organization won't be good for your own rep. They poison the well for you. If your brand is "future leader," you won't get far if you're hanging out with someone whose brand is "loser."

9. Don't Gossip

Whatever you do, don't let someone else brand you as a gossip. It's way too easy to get sucked into gossiping about coworkers, but avoid it at all costs. Say what you have to say right to the person you have a problem with. Say what you have to say out in the open at meetings instead of whispering about the people and agenda items in the hallway after the meeting ends. Gossips cannot be trusted to be managers, so they often are passed over for promotions. Gossips cannot be trusted to keep confidences, so they are left out of the critical conversations among higher-ups, who tap the employees they can trust for the primo assignments. Gossips cannot be trusted as friends, so they tend to align themselves only with other gossips. Their brand: "not going anywhere."

10. Be Accountable

When you mess up, own it. Don't blame others for your mistakes, even if others contributed to a misunderstanding or a missed commitment. Admit your failures, your shortcomings, and your missteps. Learn from them and do better next time. Every time. Nobody respects someone who blames others for her own shortcomings. But owning your shortcomings is only half of accountability. The other half is reliability. Nobody wants to work with—or promote or give a raise to—someone who is unreliable. One of the nicest compliments you can overhear bosses or coworkers giving you is, "She does what she says she will do." Make "reliable" a big part of your brand.

STEP 4. ASK FOR WHAT YOU WANT

Too many of us assume that our work speaks for itself. The idea is that if we brand ourselves as "reliable, hardworking, and deserving of the next great thing," then that "next great thing" will land in our laps. In reality, that rarely happens without a little prompting from us. That prompting takes the form of asking for what we want.

Everyone needs help with something, sometime. Nobody gets through this life all alone. Most of us rely on friends, family, coworkers, and even the kindness of strangers to get through tough times and challenging assignments.

If you're proud of a brand that sells you as someone so independent that you never need to ask for help, you might not be making the impression you mean to. Your brand—in the eyes of others—could be "doesn't get the job done because she's too stubborn to ask for help." Or "doesn't trust anyone." Or "cuts off her nose to spite her face."

That's not a good look for anyone.

It's not a good look for Joya, who has spent her entire adult life trying to prove to people that she doesn't need them.

At one point, she was working full-time, caring for three toddlers, and reeling from the unexpected news that her husband was leaving her. Then her mother got very sick, and Joya, an only child, needed to get involved with her care.

Friends, coworkers, and neighbors all volunteered to pitch in with childcare, carpools, meals, and even money. Joya said no to all of it.

"I'm OK," she told them. "I don't need anything."

The fact is, she didn't want to give up control of anything, even though there was no way she could succeed without help. She thought her brand was "strong, independent, and capable." She thought her brand was "superwoman." But the friends, coworkers, and neighbors weren't buying it. To them, Joya's brand was "stubborn, shortsighted, control freak, distrustful."

It hurt her relationships. And dealing with an impossible amount of responsibility damaged her status at work, her time with her kids, her ability to give her mom the attention she needed, and her health—both mentally and physically.

All because Joya did not want to ask for help.

Permission Mission

Can I be bold (part of my brand) and presumptuous (usually not part of my brand) and give you permission, right here and now, to ask for what you want? Can I give you permission to accept the help you need? Will you accept my permission to say no to what's too much and yes to those offering to lighten your load?

I'm on a mission to convince people—especially women—to give themselves permission to take care of themselves, to stop putting themselves in last place, and to take as much as they give.

Give yourself permission to ask for help. Sell yourself on the fact that you deserve to have what you want and need in your life.

That might be one of the hardest sales you'll ever make.

Whenever she's able to, Joya gives a lot. She's happy to watch her neighbors' children if they need her. She visits her mom almost every day. She lavishes her children with attention so they won't feel neglected as her marriage ends. She patiently advises, trains, and assists coworkers when they fall behind.

What good does the brand of "give, give, give" do you if it ruins you? Or if it leads those who know you to buy a brand that says, "I don't trust you"?

Ask for help. Most of the people you ask will be glad to return the many favors you have done for them.

Bottom line: If you don't ask, you won't get. You deserve to get everything you want and need. Ask for it.

Ask for Buy-In

The big "ask" when selling your brand is the one that invites people to buy into what you're selling.

This is an especially big ask if you're changing your brand or if you're asking someone to give you a chance to do something that stretches you out of a comfortable brand and into one that is more challenging to sell.

During the pandemic-induced lockdown of 2020 and 2021, loads of people had time to reconsider how they were spending their time. That led to the Great Resignation, when tens of millions of American employees up and quit their jobs. Some needed a break; others left the workforce permanently. But most hoped to find different jobs that would allow them to practice their passions. And in some cases, they had no experience in those new fields.

For them, rebranding was in order. People who started new businesses or changed careers had to create a new brand or add onto an existing one so they could sell themselves as capable and qualified to take on jobs that, on paper, might seem beyond their abilities.

They had to take on the enormous sales job of convincing potential employers that they would do great work, despite a lack of qualifications.

I heard of an accountant with a passion for gardening who decided to quit her corporate job and hire herself out as a landscaper.

She had a hard time convincing people she could do the job. So she transformed her own front yard into a lush, colorful showcase and then hosted a meet-and-greet at her home for her whole neighborhood. She handed out business cards and passed out flyers. By the time the event was over, she had three clients—all neighbors. They started recommending her to others, and before long, the accountant had a new brand.

A lot of employees who have quit their nine-to-five jobs have decided to work for themselves. But not everyone wants to create a business. Many have joined the gig economy as rideshare drivers, freelancers, errand runners, and others who would rather work by the gig than work for someone else. Some people rent out rooms in their homes.

Each of them needs a new brand.

When I needed a graphic designer to do a special project for me, I looked on a website full of freelancers. I found thousands of potential designers.

The one I chose, though, stood out from the rest. He impressed me by doing more than providing a 300-word bio and posting pictures of his work. I reached out to four or five candidates to ask for more info. They replied with their prices—except for the one I chose. He replied with a request for a Zoom meeting. We chatted, and he wowed me.

He has a planned brand, and he lives it. He reaches out to me from time to time to ask for work. Many of the others I saw—and many who are new to the gig economy—don't recognize the value of creating, living, and selling a brand.

Stuff your personal brand with confidence and creativity. Elevate the parts of your brand that can overcome any of its limitations.

Most importantly, give yourself permission to ask for what you want. Believe that you deserve to have what you want.

Go for it!

Five Ways Asking for Help Can Solidify Your Brand

If you want others to buy your brand, you need to ask them to. Here are five ways to use the "ask" to help you build your brand.

1. Know Your Worth

You wouldn't be creating a personal brand if you didn't believe you have something special to offer to others. You obviously believe you have the reputation, drive, talent, charisma, smarts, or potential to take your life, your career, and your success to the next level.

To me, that means you believe you deserve to get to that next level.

If you believe you deserve what's next, include that in the plan you create for solidifying your brand. Include a plan for how you will get to that next level. Include a list of people who can help you. Identify what each of those people can do to help you. Figure out how they might benefit from helping you.

Then ask for help.

Practice humility even as you make it clear you deserve what you're asking for.

Sure, the answer might be no, at least for now. But most people will respect you for having the confidence in yourself that it takes to ask for what you deserve.

If, on the other hand, you believe you do not deserve what you're asking for, you might want to reevaluate your plan to brand yourself this way. If you lack confidence in yourself, you are unlikely to successfully brand yourself as an expert, an influencer, or an up-and-comer.

2. Take the Initiative

You can ask for help, or you can ask others if they can use your help. Asking to take on that extra project, or lead the team, or fill in for a vacationing manager can plant the idea with the boss that you're someone who is willing to pitch in, to stretch yourself, and to take on more responsibility. Those are qualities that managers look for when they are promoting from within. Offering to help—asking for the chance to do something extra—will flag you as a candidate with potential, drive, and team spirit.

3. Invite Others to Follow You

During every single episode of *Vincenzo's Plate*, a fun Italian cooking show on YouTube, the host, Vincenzo, asks viewers to subscribe to his cooking channel. The more subscribers he has, of course, the more likely he is to attract sponsors. At Firehouse

Subs, a nationwide fast-food chain, as the customers are paying their bill, the cashiers ask them if they would like to round up their bill to the next dollar and donate the change to charities that represent first responders. The result: The restaurant chain has raised more than $40 million for that cause.

If you want people to follow you on social media, attend your presentations, consider you a candidate for a promotion, or otherwise help you cement your brand, ask them to. They won't if they don't want to. But many of them will be happy to.

Even before my first book, *Every Job Is a Sales Job*, hit bookstore shelves, I asked everyone I know to preorder a copy. I sent them emails. I reached out on social media. I told them about the new website, DrCindy.com. I offered them incentives like coaching packages when they bought the book. I explained how the book could help them. I asked for what I wanted. I asked for endorsements from other experts and authors.

My brand: "confident and excited about my new book." My success would depend on people who buy my book. So I asked them to buy my book.

4. Raise Your Hand

Part of branding yourself is becoming an expert about something. If you want to become the youngest partner in your law firm's history, become an expert at the kind of law you want to practice. If you want to be a social media phenom, educate yourself so well that the advice you offer online is considered unique, trustworthy, and absolutely accurate.

When someone asks, "Does anybody know how?," raise your hand. Speak up. Embrace the opportunity to be heard. Let everyone know, "I'm only 22, but I'm qualified to do this job."

Ask for the chance to show off what you know.

5. Ask for Referrals

One of the most important questions you can ask anyone is, "Will you recommend me to someone else?"

As you build your brand, your friends, family, neighbors, and colleagues will be your earliest supporters. Let them know, through your consistent behavior, what your brand is. Make sure what they say about you will be positive and will reflect your brand. Sure, you can simply tell them what to say. But their praise will be more genuine if they know all the right things to say because they see the best of you every day.

Your next most likely supporters are the clients who are satisfied with your work. Ask them to follow and recommend you as well.

Most people—even the ones who love you—won't do that on their own.

You have to ask. Then, and only then, will they post glowing reviews about you, or subscribe to your YouTube channel, or otherwise support you, just because you asked.

Displaying your brand to everyone—the people closest to you, the customers you serve, and the strangers you encounter during your day—will make it more likely that someone will put in a good word for you with the boss, pay you a compliment within earshot of your manager, post a positive Yelp review about your company that mentions your top-level service, or write you a glowing letter of recommendation when you're ready to change jobs.

Put the "Ask" to Work for Your Brand

Here's a success story that's worth imitating.

Talia worked for years as a trainer for one of the biggest banks in the world. She regularly traveled to other countries to hold workshops for employees. She loved having the opportunity to see the world and experience other cultures.

Although she wanted children, she decided to put off having a family so she could establish herself in her career and travel as much as possible. Once her daughter came, she was ready to trade her frequent flier points for midnight feedings and school plays.

She still wanted to work at the bank, though. So she came up with a plan that would allow her to continue to add value to the training team without ever getting on an airplane.

Talia had always had a knack for technology and loved to use apps and programs to design beautiful presentations with video, animation, and special effects. Her audiences appreciated her creativity, and her colleagues envied it.

So she raised her hand. She proposed that her department add a "materials manager" to the training staff—her—so she could create amazing presentations for her colleagues to use when they taught their classes.

Those coworkers loved the idea. She got them to help her pitch it to the bosses, and her new career was born.

Talia changed her brand from "trainer" to "designer," from "works on the road" to "holds down the fort." She rebranded herself as "materials expert and instructional designer."

Nobody was going to do that for her. If she hadn't raised her hand, she probably would have decided to find another employer or take a few years off from her career. But because she spoke up—asking for what she wanted after observing what her department needed—she got everything she hoped for.

You can, too. If you ask for it.

STEP 5. FOLLOW UP WITH CONSISTENCY AND GRATITUDE

All brands should incorporate room for grace, growth, and gratitude.

You may not aspire to be a social media influencer, but your brand is still important for your company and your own reputation. It would definitely suffer if you were ever photographed or videotaped losing control in public.

The best brands include a commitment to be in control of yourself. That might mean that you're thoughtful about what you say and do; that you think before you speak or act. It's a commitment that definitely calls on all of us to live our brands with consistency so we are always selling what we intend.

One example is my personal policy of not partying with clients while I'm traveling for business. I enjoy a glass of wine or champagne sometimes but not when I'm working.

Another example is from a friend who never talks about her personal life at work. Her colleagues don't even know she has five cats—a secret that's hard for a cat lover to keep—because she wants to focus on the work and never give her coworkers any reason to gossip about her.

A third scenario is from a life coach I know who handles every tense situation—including encounters with others who are upset or hurling unfair accusations—by asking questions, starting with, "What has happened to upset you?," instead of responding defensively or with accusations of her own.

Commit to your personal brand. Sustain your brand. Sell your brand. If you can't, then you may have chosen the wrong way to brand yourself.

11

Sell All of You

My gal pals and I like to meet up every now and then for drinks and appetizers at a cute little neighborhood restaurant that has a great happy hour and delicious snacks. We go straight from work, so we're usually a bit dressed up but ready to unwind from our long days.

One woman in our group, Rosella, is single, and the rest of us are married. So we were all happy for Rosella when a very handsome, casually dressed man started chatting with her at the bar while she was waiting for a refill.

Rosella, dressed in a smart business suit appropriate for her job as a receptionist, thought the two of them were really hitting it off until he asked her, "Don't you ever just wear a casual sweater and comfortable jeans?"

"Yes, all the time, when I'm not working," she replied. "I just left my office; that's why I'm dressed up."

But the handsome man had formed a snap judgment based on how she was dressed and on the bit of leftover workday stress he detected as they spoke.

He said, "You seem so formal to me, like you're still at work. I like to relax and have fun when I leave my office. You seem like you're someone who is always 'on.'"

His loss. Rosella is a lot of fun. But like most of us, it takes her a little while to shift gears from work to play at the end of a rough day.

I call those gears "facets." Our personalities have multiple facets. So must our brands. And one of the keys to selling ourselves is to be able to quickly elevate the facet of our brand that is just right for the situation we find ourselves in.

Rosella didn't elevate her social facet quickly and lost the opportunity to connect with the handsome man.

But seriously, in my opinion, it was his loss. Snap judgments usually are inaccurate.

Still, lesson learned. We have to become adept at knowing which facet to showcase when and with whom.

Sometimes we need to elevate a part of our brand that we don't often show to people.

If Rosella had elevated the "fun" part of her brand and tamped down her workday brand a little bit quicker, the handsome man would have seen what I see in Rosella so often: a quick wit, a kind word, an interest in travel and art, and a great conversationalist.

Rosella wasn't prepared to elevate a facet of her brand that didn't say "all work, no play." In that moment, she sold herself short.

COUNT YOUR FACETS

Like a cut diamond, we shine a little more brilliantly when you look at us in one light than when you catch us in another.

Like Rosella's, my brand has "professional" written all over it. I dress and behave professionally when I coach clients in person, on Zoom, or on the phone. I'm professional around my own team and vendors. Anyone who meets me at a conference or a speaking engagement will, I hope, immediately get the impression that I'm professional through and through.

And when I meet a client for a quick dinner during a convention or after a meeting, I'm still professional. I might wear flats and a sweater instead of pumps and a blazer, but I keep the conversation light and not too personal.

Those occasions are fun and friendly. But my behavior is still professional. I stay on brand. I live my brand every minute that I'm working or I'm with a work-related colleague.

But when I get home, I throw on my sweats and comfy slippers and talk about my dog and my frustrations and my hopes and dreams with my husband or family or closest friends. With those people, I'm personal and vulnerable.

And when I go to a restaurant for dinner with my husband and friends, I dress up a little, sometimes in a fun dress or slacks with a nice sweater—and I ask our dinner companions a lot of questions and talk about current events and pets and vacations. On these occasions, I'm conversational and—I hope—interesting without getting too personal or too businesslike.

I am naturally curious, and I really love getting to know people and hear their stories. When I go on vacation and meet strangers, I try to find out as much as I can about them without prying, and I let them get to know a little bit about me, without being too revealing.

In different situations, I elevate different parts of my brand.

My brand has so many facets. As a professional, my brand includes "polished, confident, well educated, published author, keynote speaker, experienced coach and trainer, saleswoman." Personally, I love scary movies; I have a dog; I'm married; I enjoy eating in restaurants; I like to travel; I like to dance. And no matter what the situation, I try to be kind, attentive, helpful, and thoughtful—which intersect with all the facets of my brand.

I could list 100 things about me that the people I meet at work may never know unless it happens to come up in a conversation that we have something personal in common. And I could list 100 things that I do at work that even my closest friends don't know because we don't spend a lot of time talking about work.

You have those lists, too. And no matter how specific your brand plan is—it might focus on your professional goals rather than personal facets, for instance—everything on that unwritten list is another facet of your brand.

If it's part of you, it's part of your brand.

Take advantage of that.

Being well rounded comes in handy all the time. So even if you live the main part of your brand every day—the professional, for instance—keep all those other facets on hand in case elevating one of them might suit you in the moment.

In Rosella's case, her sense of humor or her great conversation skills might have made her more interesting to the handsome man—someone she found interesting.

In my case, I dusted off a part of my brand when I visited the South for some workshops, as I described in an earlier chapter. I elevated a facet of my brand—I lived in the South when I was young. That helped me connect with a couple of women I met at an event I spoke at.

My friend Sam is a salesman by occupation and a wine connoisseur by hobby. He elevates the connoisseur facet of his brand often as he establishes rapport and trust with clients who are just getting to know him. If they're having lunch and a client orders a glass of wine, he offers what he knows about the vintage. If a group can't decide which wine to order for the table, he identifies himself as someone who can help with that.

If it doesn't come up, generally he doesn't bring it up. But he does when he thinks it might move a conversation along or make a social occasion more fun or help him make a sale.

Sam, like me, like Rosella, and like you, is a multifaceted person. He has a brand that includes many facets—although you might never find out about most of them, even if you work with him every day.

Our second- and third-tier facets are there to elevate when we need them. They don't interfere with what our professional brand shows to the world. Instead, they can help us make a good impression during specific meetings, conversations, or situations where professional isn't enough.

What follows are some examples of situations that sometimes call on us to elevate a part of our brand that we don't rely on every day.

The Job Interview

Having a personal brand helps us put our best foot forward in every situation. When it's time for a job interview, though, we need to pull out all the stops.

A job interview requires a level of formality that we might not live day in and day out, even at work. We dress up for a job interview, even if the job we're in now allows us to wear jeans to work.

In this situation, we elevate the part of our brand that says, "I'm ready for the next level." So you dress as if you already have the job. Even if you're usually shy or reluctant, you elevate your confidence, your conversational skills, and your expertise as you answer the interviewer's questions. Even if you're the life of the party after hours, you elevate the controlled, professional part of your brand here and now. Even if you're known as someone who posts about every encounter on social media, you elevate your common sense and put your phone away so you can give the interviewer your full attention.

One client described how he unexpectedly found himself elevating his inner computer geek during an interview for a job as a teller at a bank. He knew he would have to elevate the part of his brand that he believed qualified him for the job: "friendly, polite, efficient, and good with people and money." But when the manager's computer screen froze during the interview and she was unable to pull up a form she needed my client to fill out, he asked if he could take a look.

He was able to fix the problem. It turns out that the bank was short-staffed and the manager had to double as an IT troubleshooter for her small team, and she really didn't know how.

My client got a job there, but not as a teller. It turns out that friendly, polite, efficient, and good with people and money, plus savvy about computers, qualified him to fill another opening—for an assistant manager.

The Performance Review

If part of your brand is "charming," job interviews with strangers are probably easy for you. But you can't charm your way through a performance review with a boss who probably knows both your best and your worst.

Here is a situation that requires you to elevate a part of your brand that you might deliberately keep hidden: the part that shows your pride and allows you to brag a little bit about your value and your accomplishments.

Humility is a truly important and worthwhile part of the personal brand of anyone for whom that quality comes naturally. It's not a bad idea for people who love to talk and brag about themselves to practice humility as well so they don't come off as egomaniacs.

But alongside your instinct to let your work and work ethic speak for themselves comes a need to toot your own horn during performance reviews, requests for a raise, and other situations that have the potential to benefit you.

Don't let your brand sell you short by neglecting to shine your brightest when you have conversations with managers and others who have the authority to decide how much money you earn, which projects you will be assigned, whether you get a promotion, or even which cubicle you will sit in.

Elevate the part of your brand that knows what you're worth and isn't afraid to ask for it.

If that is not part of your brand—not even hidden way down deep someplace in your brand—work on that.

As you learned in the previous chapter, asking for what you want is one of the five critical steps you need to take if you want to make a sale. In a performance review, you are selling yourself. You need to ask for what you want.

First, figure out what that is. For example:

1. Recognition?

If so, ask if your boss knows about each great thing you did. Elevate the part of your brand that shows others you are confident you're doing a good job and are ready for the next one. Elevate the part of your brand that displays your pride in your good work and abilities. You don't have to brag. But you do have to speak up. Elevate the facets of your brand that you're usually too humble to show off and put them to work for you now.

2. Good Performance Review?

Ask for a raise. Ask for a promotion. Explain why you deserve them. Explain how you have earned them. Again, you can do this in a humble way, simply by stating the facts and explaining the details. You don't have to say you're the world's greatest employee. Instead, give your manager the evidence she needs to realize that you are. Don't make the mistake of assuming your manager already knows you have done this excellent work. Don't assume she knows you want a raise or a promotion. Assumptions sell you short.

3. Counteroffer?

Muster up the "bold" in your brand and tell your manager you'll stay if she can match the offer you have from that competitor. There's no guarantee that she will pony up the money. But if you don't ask, you won't get.

The First Date

Besides a job interview, a first date is probably the situation that requires you to make your absolute best first impression on another person.

This is when someone whose brand is "shy" needs to elevate whatever glimmer of outgoing is hiding beneath so many stronger qualities within his or her personal brand.

Try this: Think of a first date as a sale. You're selling your date on liking you, on wanting to spend more time with you, on having a nice time with you, and on finding you interesting.

What part of your brand will convince your date to say yes to that?

Is it your dry sense of humor? Bring it to the forefront. The story you tell that everyone seems to enjoy? Tell it. An interesting description of your unique hobby? Try it out.

Or maybe part of your shy charm is that you don't like to talk about yourself, but people tell you that you ask great questions. Elevate your inner curiosity and engage your date in a way that will make him or her the center of the conversation. Show off the "good listener" part of your brand. Respond with comments that show you're listening, engaged, and interested.

"Curious," "good listener," "engaged," and "interested" aren't bad brands for a first date.

In fact, if your brand is "naturally outgoing" and "never runs out of things to say," it's not a bad idea to tamp down that part of your brand to let your date talk. Elevate your "curious, good listener" and watch that first date turn into a second one.

The Favor

Whenever you ask someone for a favor, elevate the part of your brand that will show you in the best light for what you're asking.

Recently when I called for an Uber, a driver showed up in a fancy black car—even though I had requested regular service. He got out of the car, and I saw he was wearing a suit and tie. He opened the door and used a tiny broom to sweep off the car seat. He waited for me to climb in, and he closed the door.

Once we were on the road, he asked me to choose a radio station for us to listen to during our trip, which took about 20 minutes. He offered me a bottle of water. He asked me what I was doing that day. He gauged whether I wanted to talk.

I did, and I was grateful that he did, too.

By the time we reached my destination, I learned that he quit his construction job a year earlier because of an injury and wanted to make it as a full-time driver. Over the year, he had driven an older Honda, which he kept very clean. But when riders rated him, they typically assigned him four stars instead of five.

So he asked some friends to let him drive them, and he asked them to rate him honestly. Four out of five stars.

The experience, they said, was good. The car was clean. He's good company. There's nothing wrong with four stars, they told him.

So he asked them what he could do to get five stars. Their response: Set yourself apart with a bigger car and some extras, like bottled water.

And that's what he did. He bought a used sedan, and he washes it every single day. He started treating his riders as if they had hired a limousine. His ratings soared.

Before I got out of the car, my driver asked me if he had given me five-star service that day. I said he had. Then he asked me for a favor: He asked me to give him a five-star rating.

That's exactly what I did.

The Unexpected Opportunity

You never know when an opportunity will arise that will give you a chance to get what you want if you're quick on your feet and elevate your brand to suit the occasion.

I never expected, when I had just started writing my first book, *Every Job Is a Sales Job*, that I would, simply by chance, meet someone who works for a book publisher. I wound up sitting next to her on an airplane on my way back from a convention.

I can thank my brand plan for the outfit I chose to wear that day: a dark pantsuit and conservative pumps. For an airplane ride, I think I might be more comfortable in my favorite sweats and broken-in sneakers, but I always dress up on travel days so—just in case a professional opportunity presents itself—I'll look my best and put forward my brand of professionalism.

She initiated the conversation by asking me what kind of work I did. I showcased my best coach/trainer/saleswoman/business owner brand. Then I asked about her.

She worked for a publishing company.

Me? I was hoping to publish my first book.

Change of plans. Dust off the aspiring author facet of my brand. Do it quickly. No problem. I was prepared for this day, even if it never came.

A great conversation followed. She gave me tons of useful advice—and her business card. We've been in touch over the years, and she continues to give me great advice.

It's possible that this woman would have taken me just as seriously if I had dressed for a Saturday afternoon at home instead of for a chance business conversation. But maybe not. My plan is to always be prepared.

What would you do if you happened to sit in the airplane seat next to the exact person who can help you make your dreams come true? Stop wondering. Plan for it.

Most of us have aspirations beyond the job we currently hold. Those aspirations might be based on talents, skills, or desires that we don't tap into much in our current jobs. All those facets are part of your brand at a lower tier than the personal brand you live daily.

Don't let them get rusty. Take some time to plan for potential opportunities. Know which part of your brand you will elevate and what you will say if:

- You want to work for Apple and you're the only person in an elevator when CEO Tim Cook walks into it. You've got two minutes.
- Your aunt tells you she is doing business with a venture capitalist who specializes in transportation startups—and you have a solid plan for a luxury car service. She's reluctant to impose on her client.
- You want a letter of recommendation from a professor who knows the head of the local LGBTQIA association, where you hope to work as an intern. You see her across the room at a fundraising dinner. She gave you a D in her diversity class.
- The woman you've been too timid to ask out despite your yearlong crush signs up for the neighborhood softball

team, and you're the catcher. She's been flirting with the left fielder.

Plan for it. Don't forget that you're a multifaceted person who is awesome at more than one thing. Elevate your many facets as situations arise that make certain facets more relevant than other facets.

Moments That Matter

Those are moments that matter. Be prepared for them, or you will remember them as missed opportunities. I go into depth about this in *Every Job Is a Sales Job.*

Not all opportunities to elevate little-used facets of your brand are impromptu, however.

Some of the most important moments of our lives give us time to plan for them.

The job interview is one of them. So is an invitation to make the best man's toast at your brother's wedding, or to deliver the eulogy for a beloved uncle, or to speak about a valued mentor and boss at her retirement party.

These are occasions when your polish, professionalism, and experience will intersect with the part of your brand that makes you a good friend, a caring sibling, or a grateful recipient of whatever time, love, and advice the special people in your life have showered you with.

You might need to override your tendency to make snarky, off-the-cuff jokes—something that you're proud to showcase as part of your personal brand—with the barely used facet that shows you know the importance of decorum and respect at the retirement party. You might be all-business at work—a brand that lets your teammates know the work is going to get done—but you'll have to elevate your softer, compassionate side for a eulogy.

Don't suppress any sides of your personality, even though some of them might not be appropriate all the time. Like Bikini Girl from Chapter 2, you need to consider the people who are watching and what you want them to see.

Then shine a bright spotlight on that facet to make sure everyone sees what you want them to see.

WHILE YOU WERE SLEEPING

A discussion about your multifaceted personal brand wouldn't be complete without addressing which facets you want to shine on social media.

Sometimes you make your first impression on someone while you're sleeping.

What I mean is that in this 24/7 digital world, anyone could be viewing your digital presence at any time, even when you can't control the circumstances or decide which facet to elevate for those particular people.

A single facet of your brand probably will not impress everyone who views your social media sites or your website if you have one.

So make your social media presence multifaceted, too.

But beware: Be consistent. Don't, for example, create two completely separate brands on two different social media platforms—like Bikini Girl did with her "model" and "documentarian" brands. Instead, find the facets of your brand that will portray you at your very best.

Sure, you might need to leave a few things out. I don't post photos of my precious dog Biscuit or my family vacations on social media, for instance. But I do merge my "professional/coach/trainer/business owner/author" brand with my "helpful/kind/reliable" brand. The result: a brand that I would be proud to show anyone, in person or online.

I've said this a number of times in this book. If you think you can have a personal social media brand that's separate from your professional social media brand, you're mistaken. People can see anything online if they look hard enough, despite privacy settings.

Choose your "whole you" brand for social media and save your "for friends only" brand for in person.

It all points back to knowing what you are selling. What are you selling online that you would never want to sell in person? Whatever that is, it's time to let it go.

Private Parts

Some facets of your personality and history might not make it into your personal brand.

You might have a bad habit or a behavior that you're not proud of, and so you don't want to share that with the world.

You might have done something in your past that you would rather forget and that you would rather people don't find out.

You might have a secret that you've never shared with anyone or with only your closest friend or spouse.

You might have some pain from an experience or a loss or a trauma that is yours alone and nobody else's business.

Your brand is who you are in the eyes of anyone who knows you or knows anything about you. It's how you present yourself in public and with the individuals you interact with.

But you don't have to tell everything. You don't have to show everything. Having a personal brand does not mean you can't have privacy around the things you consider private.

As you create your brand, decide what you want to keep private. As you live your brand, decide if you ever want to elevate those parts of you and make them public. As you sell your brand, be careful not to intrude on your own sense of what's too personal—even if it will help you make your sale; even if it will help you sell yourself.

For a lot of people, one of the facets of their brands is "private me." They don't reveal it. They don't live it. They don't sell it. They keep it, just for themselves.

Even some celebrities who make their living in public abide by this unwritten rule of personal branding and carefully guard their privacy.

Megastar Julia Roberts, for example, moved to New Mexico so she could live a private life with her husband and children when she wasn't working on or promoting a film. You won't read much about actors Matt Damon, Cate Blanchett, or Denzel Washington in supermarket tabloids because they don't put their personal business out there for everyone to comment on. It's a good bet that you didn't know superstar Kate Winslet has been married three times and has one child with each husband. She doesn't talk about it publicly.

You don't have to, either. Some people call themselves "an open book," but chances are they are only open about what they want others to know. The rest is private.

That's not to say you shouldn't let others know you. But the point of creating, living, and selling your personal brand is to have a way to present yourself to others as your very best self. Revealing personal failures or unflattering details about yourself won't help you do that.

I've revealed a lot of details about my life and my brand to you on the pages of this book. But I'm fairly reserved about what I choose to share.

Even my team at work doesn't know much about my childhood or my family; those are memories and relationships that I want to keep private, and I would never try to use them to achieve professional success. Since that's my mindset, that information is not relevant to anybody, and certainly not to everybody.

As you create, live, and sell your personal brand, consider what you want to reveal and what you want to keep private. Make it part of your brand to keep your private side private. And just as you have committed to showcasing your brand by living it every day, commit to keeping certain personal details to yourself as a way to protect yourself and your brand.

Brand Protection

Brands do need protecting.

If there ever comes a time when you are unable to live your brand—or live up to it—because you need a break, take one.

Sometimes we just don't feel like ourselves. We get the blues; we have an emotional setback because of a loss or a disappointment; we burn out. When that happens, it can be hard to be at our best every minute of the day. And when that gets hard, we run the risk of going off brand.

As we've seen in prior chapters, going off brand can damage your reputation. It can raise questions among people who counted on you to be one way—and now you're showing an unexpected, unflattering side of yourself.

Before you get to that time, take a brand break.

Remember Shawn Anderson, the news anchorman from Chapter 5? He described his brand as "me, plus 10 percent." He acknowledged that he has days when he simply can't find that extra 10 percent. On those days, he stays out of the public eye.

He's a smart man. He knows that if he slips, it doesn't matter that he can explain it away as a bad day, a reaction to stress, or another reasonable excuse. All that matters is that people have witnessed an off-brand moment, and that's what they will remember.

He stays out of the public eye because he understands the value of consistency in branding. And he understands that a single off-brand incident can lead others to question his authenticity. It can damage his brand—and his radio station's brand.

A great example of this comes from a *New York Times Magazine* article about Laurie Santos, a professor at Yale University who teaches about happiness. She has a podcast called *The Happiness Lab*, and her students call her the "happiness professor."

She recently took a leave of absence.

The student newspaper reported that she took the leave because she is burned out. The *Times* reporter who interviewed her asked, "If the happiness professor is feeling burned out, what hope is there for the rest of us?"

Her answer might sell you on the need to know when your brand is burning you out—and to remove yourself from view when it does.

Professor Santos responded: "I took a leave of absence because I'm trying not to burn out. I know the signs of burnout. It's not like one morning you wake up, and you're burnt. You're noticing more emotional exhaustion. You're noticing what researchers call depersonalization. You get annoyed with people more quickly. You immediately assume someone's intentions are bad. You start feeling ineffective.

"I'd be lying if I said I wasn't noticing those things in myself . . . so it's not a story of, 'Even the happiness professor isn't happy.' This is a story of, 'I'm making these changes now so I don't get to that point of being burned out.' I see it as a positive."

I also see it as a positive. Nobody can perform at the highest level all day every day without the occasional break, any more than we can work nonstop with no weekends off or no vacations ever. We're people, after all, and although our brands help us showcase our superpowers, we're not superhuman.

We get tired, even exhausted. And we go off brand. The jetlagged woman with the nice brand is rude to an airport worker when her bag is lost. The young man with the polished professional brand shows up at a business meeting wearing jeans and flip-flops and sporting a three-day-old stubble on his face. The social media influencer who preaches clean eating succumbs to the temptation of a creamy éclair, and someone catches it on video.

Exhaustion, stress, grief, and other extreme emotions and conditions are bad for brands. As soon as you start showing symptoms, stay home!

To protect your brand, you have to live it consistently. If you reach a point where that doesn't seem possible, take a brand break. Remove yourself from your daily routine. Surround yourself with people who know you and love you. Let your guard down—in private. Rest. Recover. Regroup.

You owe it to your brand. You owe it to yourself. You owe it to the people who are counting on you to be the best you that you can be.

EPILOGUE

Leaving a Legacy

"Leaving a legacy," for most of us, conjures images of presidents or queens or wealthy philanthropists whose names will be on libraries, colleges, and even airports as a reward for the good work they did during their time on earth. Some believe that their children are their legacy; that those they have raised and taught and left behind will carry on the good family name.

Your legacy is what people will remember about you long after you're gone—from this life or even from a job you've had for a long time or a neighborhood where you lived for decades or a career you retired from.

What will people remember about you?

What would you like them to remember?

In the absence of a very public accomplishment—like a series of bestselling books or a term in elected office or an invention that has a positive impact on scores of people—your legacy will reveal itself through the way you live day by day.

People will remember you for your kindness or your quick wit or your way with children or your love of animals. Or they will remember you for your short temper, your closed-mindedness, your selfishness, or your unfriendliness.

It's also possible that your legacy will hinge on a single kindness—like the time you put your own safety at risk to save someone else—or an isolated bad act, like the time, in a fit of anger, you threatened your neighbor's yappy dog.

It's up to you.

Few of us will have a crew of planners and public relations pros to cement our legacy by building us a library to memorialize our every word or erecting a monument so our face will never be forgotten. But all of us have a personal brand that we live and sell every day by the way we behave and treat others.

And that is what will become our legacy.

You get to choose.

When we plan our brands, it's natural to consider how we want others to view us right now. We might also factor in how a personal brand might propel us into the next position we want at work or into a seat at the table where the cool kids sit.

In fact, we should look much farther into the future when we decide how we will live our lives. We should think beyond our reputation today and consider the legacy we are creating for ourselves.

How will the actions you take today and the next day and the next affect how people will remember you once you've left the building?

I would be delighted if, when I retire from consulting, writing, and teaching, I still get letters from readers and former students who tell me that my books or my classes changed their lives.

But I would be equally pleased if the only thing people associate with my name is helpfulness.

I'm a helpful person by nature. In fact, I sometimes refer to myself as a "helpaholic." Helpful is core to my brand. It's ingrained in my day. It's who I am and how I'm known.

I would be honored for helpful to be my legacy.

What makes you proud about your personal brand? About the way you live your life? About who and how you are day in and day out?

Think about that now, as you create your personal brand or as you rebrand to suit a change in your life. Think about it now, while you have time to live the qualities you want others to appreciate about you.

Think about it before you reach a point in your life where you look back and wish you had branded yourself differently.

Think about your legacy.

It's a useful exercise to write a tribute to yourself—something you wish a colleague or friend would say at your retirement party or—if we want to be a little bit morbid—at your funeral.

Then write another one, but this time, write it with brutal honesty rather than with wishful thinking. What, in reality, would people say about you?

What do they say about you now when they think you're not listening?

I saw a fun pillow at a friend's house, embroidered with this sentiment: "Be the person your dog thinks you are."

Your pet most likely thinks you're kind and reliable, loving and protective.

That's not a bad legacy.

Be the person you want to be remembered as. Create a personal brand that not only will get you what you want today, but will leave others with the memories you hope they will have of you when your time is up.

Create that brand and then live it. Create that brand and then sell it.

Create that brand and create the legacy that you want to leave.

Index

About the Author

© LIVING NOTES PHOTOGRAPHY

Dr. Cindy McGovern is internationally renowned as a business and motivational speaker and is an expert in sales, leadership, and communication. Known as the First Lady of Sales, Dr. Cindy is the author of the *Wall Street Journal* bestseller *Every Job Is a Sales Job: How to Use the Art of Selling to Win at Work*. As the founder and CEO of Orange Leaf Consulting, Dr. Cindy has helped hundreds of companies grow their businesses by creating a culture in which all employees, regardless of job title, embrace sales as a natural way to help themselves and others.

Through coaching and training, Dr. Cindy helps people get what they want and need out of life by using sales skills every day.

A former college professor, Dr. Cindy holds a doctorate in organizational communication and is passionate about helping others realize that every interaction is a potential sale.

Contact her at DrCindy.com or @1stLadyofSales.